Canvas Cookbook

Over 80 simple but creative and structured recipes
to explore the capabilities of HTML5 Canvas

Bhushan Purushottam Joshi

BIRMINGHAM - MUMBAI

Canvas Cookbook

First published: April 2016

Production reference: 1260416

Published by Packt Publishing Ltd.
Livery Place
35 Livery Street
Birmingham B3 2PB, UK.

ISBN 978-1-78528-489-2

www.packtpub.com

Credits

Author
Bhushan Purushottam Joshi

Reviewer
Anirudh Prabhu

Commissioning Editor
Dipika Gaonkar

Acquisition Editor
Tushar Gupta

Content Development Editor
Arshiya Ayaz Umer

Technical Editor
Rupali Shrawane

Copy Editor
Charlotte Carneiro

Project Coordinator
Kinjal Bari

Proofreader
Safis Editing

Indexer
Rekha Nair

Production Coordinator
Aparna Bhagat

Cover Work
Aparna Bhagat

About the Author

Bhushan Purushottam Joshi is a teacher of computer science and has around 11 years of experience in teaching. He started his career as a programmer in a software firm but found true joy in teaching. He is a teacher by choice and not by chance. He teaches computer science courses such as MCA, MSc IT, BSc IT, and BSc CS at various colleges in Mumbai. He is a master at presenting technical as well as conceptual subjects in the most simplified manner. He has exemplary skill at relating daily life examples to technical concepts, which facilitates understanding of the subject matter. He enjoys teaching technical as well as conceptual subjects such as web design, Java, C#, C++, operating systems, computer networks, data structures, and ethical hacking. He is quite popular and appreciated among students for his able guidance in their project work.

Canvas Cookbook is his first sincere attempt to present the usage of HTML5 Canvas in conjunction with JavaScript and CSS to build simple and crisp recipes.

I would like to thank one of my students, Aditya Chavan, who recommended my name for the book and from there onwards, this pleasant journey of book writing commenced. I would like to thank my wife, Kalyani, and son, Soham, for giving me maximum support while writing this book. I am thankful to my father, mother, and parents-in-law for being there always and reducing the burden of my daily chores.

I would like to dedicate this book to my late grandfather, Shri Dattatray Karmarkar, who always showed an undaunted faith in me.

About the Reviewer

Anirudh Prabhu is a UI Developer with more than 5 years of experience. He specializes in HTML, CSS, JavaScript, jQuery, Sass, LESS, and Twitter Bootstrap. Additionally, he has been associated with *Packt Publishing* and *Apress* as a tech reviewer for several titles. He is the author of *Beginning CSS Preprocessors, Apress Publications*. In addition to aforementioned skills, he has experience of CoffeeScript and AngularJS. Anirudh has also been involved in building training material for HTML, CSS, and jQuery for twenty19 (`www.twenty19.com`), which is a portal for providing training for freshers and interns.

www.PacktPub.com

eBooks, discount offers, and more

Did you know that Packt offers eBook versions of every book published, with PDF and ePub files available? You can upgrade to the eBook version at www.PacktPub.com and as a print book customer, you are entitled to a discount on the eBook copy. Get in touch with us at customercare@packtpub.com for more details.

At www.PacktPub.com, you can also read a collection of free technical articles, sign up for a range of free newsletters and receive exclusive discounts and offers on Packt books and eBooks.

https://www2.packtpub.com/books/subscription/packtlib

Do you need instant solutions to your IT questions? PacktLib is Packt's online digital book library. Here, you can search, access, and read Packt's entire library of books.

Why Subscribe?

- ▸ Fully searchable across every book published by Packt
- ▸ Copy and paste, print, and bookmark content
- ▸ On demand and accessible via a web browser

Table of Contents

Preface   v

Chapter 1: Paths and Text   1
- Introduction   2
- Drawing lines   2
- Drawing horizontal, vertical, and assorted lines   7
- Drawing joins   10
- Drawing arc1   12
- Drawing arc2   15
- Drawing a quadratic curve   19
- Drawing a rainbow   21
- Drawing a Bezier curve   22
- Drawing a flag   24
- Drawing text   27
- Drawing 3D text with shadows   29
- Adding shadows to objects   32
- Drawing a house   34

Chapter 2: Shapes and Composites   39
- Introduction   39
- Drawing rectangles   40
- Drawing triangles   42
- Drawing circles   44
- Drawing gradients   46
- Working with custom shapes and styles   50
- Demonstrating translation, rotation, and scaling   52
- Drawing an ellipse   55
- Saving and restoring canvas state   56
- Demonstrating composites   59
- Drawing a mouse   63

Chapter 3: Animation   67

Introduction   67
Creating an animation class   68
Demonstrating acceleration   68
Demonstrating gravity   71
Animating a line   73
Animating text   76
Animating a clock   78
Animating a solar system   83
Animating particles   86
Animating a particle fountain   90
Animating a rain effect   93
Animating a snow effect   97

Chapter 4: Images and Videos   101

Introduction   101
Drawing and cropping an image   102
Rendering effects to images   105
Drawing a mirror image   108
Clipping a path   110
Animated clipping   112
Converting canvas to image and back to canvas   115
Working with videos   118
Rendering effects to videos   119
Creating a pixelated image focus   122

Chapter 5: Interactivity through Events   127

Introduction   127
Working with mouse coordinates   128
Making a face smile   130
Detecting a point in a path   133
Simulating car movements   136
Dragging and dropping   139
Combining events and animation   142
Demonstrating a touch event   145

Chapter 6: Creating Graphs and Charts   147

Introduction   147
Drawing the axes   148
Drawing a simple equation   152
Drawing a sinusoidal wave   155

Drawing a line graph 158
Drawing a bar graph 162
Drawing a pie chart 166

Chapter 7: 3D Modeling 169

Introduction 169
Rendering 3D objects 170
Drawing 3D cubes 174
Drawing a 3D cylinder and a cone 179
Drawing a 3D sphere and a torus 182
Drawing 3D text decorated by particles 185
Drawing a panorama 189
Drawing a snowman 192

Chapter 8: Game Development 197

Introduction 197
Understanding the gaming states 198
Drawing on canvas 199
Playing some music 201
Using sprites from the sprite sheet 203
Demonstrating animation 205
Demonstrating collision 207
Demonstrating physics 210
Game 1 – Fruit Basket 212
Game 2 – Catapult 216

Chapter 9: Interoperability and Deployment 223

Introduction 223
Understanding interoperability 224
Styling text and background using CSS 224
Deploying a game on Android mobile 226

Index 233

Preface

The world of gaming is very competitive, and day by day the technology is evolving and making things easier for users. HTML5 is a recent standard, which is flexible, interactive, and portable. It is supported by most browsers. This makes HTML5 a good language for developing applications with a wider reach.

The Canvas element in HTML5 is quite interesting as it allows programmers to render whatever they can imagine. Canvas allows users to draw 2D and 3D objects and render animation. HTML5 Canvas is therefore a suitable technology for developing applications and games for a variety of devices.

However, without a scripting language, HTML5 Canvas, is of limited use. A scripting language such as JavaScript is necessary to make use of HTML5 Canvas and is at the heart of any application or game.

Any application without style is an ordinary application that will not catch the eye of a user. Styling is important when it comes to developing applications commercially. It adds richness to the application. **CSS** helps developers do this.

This book is all about the usage of HTML5 Canvas, JavaScript, and CSS in the development of various recipes. The book starts with basic drawings on Canvas, graduates to animation and 3D rendering, and culminates with the development of games that can run on different devices. The recipes in each chapter are simple and crisp. The last few chapters exhibit the usage of third-party libraries such as `Three.js` and `Phaser.js`.

All recipes are supported with a precise explanation to inspire the reader to develop his or her own recipes.

What this book covers

Chapter 1, Paths and Text, is a simple chapter where you can view basic recipes to draw lines, arcs, curves, and text. It introduces the use of the Canvas API to render drawings.

Chapter 2, Shapes and Composites, introduces various shapes such as triangles, rectangles, circles, and ellipses. Coloring and styling is also demonstrated in a few recipes. You will find here exciting recipes rendering styled text and various types of composite.

Chapter 3, Animation, uses the drawings made in the previous chapter and adds some actions to them. It introduces a systematic approach toward animation. It covers basic movements such as linear motion, acceleration, oscillation, and its implementation through impressive recipes.

Chapter 4, Images and Videos, reveals the rendering of images and videos. The recipes show the clipping and cropping of images. Images on canvas are the basic foundation for any application or game.

Chapter 5, Interactivity through Events, introduces event handling. It encompasses events captured through input devices such as the mouse, keyboard, and touch. You will be able to create a simple game at the end of this chapter.

Chapter 6, Creating Graphs and Charts, displays different types of graph and chart. These are ideal for any data presentation. Here, I will show you to draw simple x and y axes and then plot different equations on them. You will learn to draw a bar chart and a pie chart.

Chapter 7, 3D Modeling, will show you the rendering of 3D objects. It will introduce you to an open source library named Three.js, used to draw various shapes such as cubes, spheres, cylinders, and toruses.

Chapter 8, Game Development, explains the complete procedure for developing a game. It is time to assemble all the nuts and bolts. I introduce here another open source library Phaser.js, which is one of the popular libraries for game development. You will learn various game stages, playing audio, creating and using sprites, and much more.

Chapter 9, Interoperability and Compatibility, is just an extension to the previous chapter, which highlights the deployment of the game on a mobile phone. You will encounter the use of CSS to enhance the look and feel of the game.

What you need for this book

The software required for trying out the recipes in this book are listed here:

- ▸ Any browser that supports HTML5 Canvas and WebGL. I used Chrome Version 48.0.2564.116 m.
- ▸ A web server to execute a few recipes that render images and video. I used IIS7.

- ▸ Third-party libraries Three.js and Phaser.js.
- ▸ You can create a repository on GitHub and register at `build.phonegap.com` to build your own applications for mobile phones.

All of these are easily available, and you can try the recipes on any platform. However, I tested the recipes on Windows 7 Professional.

Who this book is for

The book is intended for readers with a preliminary knowledge of JavaScript and CSS. Whether you're a beginner or expert in this technology, the book provides recipes to help you build your own application, presentation, or game.

Sections

In this book, you will find several headings that appear frequently (Getting ready, How to do it, How it works, There's more, and See also).

To give clear instructions on how to complete a recipe, we use these sections as follows:

How to do it...

This section contains the steps required to follow the recipe.

How it works...

This section usually consists of a detailed explanation of what happened in the previous section.

There's more...

This section suggests the reader to make changes in the recipes and thereby develop his/her own recipes.

Conventions

In this book, you will find a number of text styles that distinguish between different kinds of information. Here are some examples of these styles and an explanation of their meaning.

Code words in text, database table names, folder names, filenames, file extensions, pathnames, dummy URLs, user input, and Twitter handles are shown as follows: "The on load property is responsible to invoke the `init()` function."

A block of code is set as follows:

```html
<html>
<head>
  <title>Simple Lines</title>
    <script type="text/javascript">
      var can;
      var ctx;
```

When we wish to draw your attention to a particular part of a code block, the relevant lines or items are set in bold:

```
function drawHorizontalLines()
    {
        xs=10;  ys=10;xe=100; ye=10;
        c="teal";  w=2;
        //draw 10 lines
```

New terms and **important words** are shown in bold. Words that you see on the screen, for example, in menus or dialog boxes, appear in the text like this: "If your browser doesn't support Canvas then it will display **Your browser doesn't support Canvas** as mentioned in the Canvas element of the HTML code."

 Warnings or important notes appear in a box like this.

 Tips and tricks appear like this.

Reader feedback

Feedback from our readers is always welcome. Let us know what you think about this book—what you liked or disliked. Reader feedback is important for us as it helps us develop titles that you will really get the most out of.

To send us general feedback, simply e-mail feedback@packtpub.com, and mention the book's title in the subject of your message.

If there is a topic that you have expertise in and you are interested in either writing or contributing to a book, see our author guide at www.packtpub.com/authors.

Customer support

Now that you are the proud owner of a Packt book, we have a number of things to help you to get the most from your purchase.

Downloading the example code

You can download the example code files for this book from your account at `http://www.packtpub.com`. If you purchased this book elsewhere, you can visit `http://www.packtpub.com/support` and register to have the files e-mailed directly to you.

You can download the code files by following these steps:

1. Log in or register to our website using your e-mail address and password.
2. Hover the mouse pointer on the **SUPPORT** tab at the top.
3. Click on **Code Downloads & Errata**.
4. Enter the name of the book in the **Search** box.
5. Select the book for which you're looking to download the code files.
6. Choose from the drop-down menu where you purchased this book from.
7. Click on **Code Download**.

You can also download the code files by clicking on the **Code Files** button on the book's webpage at the Packt Publishing website. This page can be accessed by entering the book's name in the **Search** box. Please note that you need to be logged in to your Packt account.

Once the file is downloaded, please make sure that you unzip or extract the folder using the latest version of:

- WinRAR / 7-Zip for Windows
- Zipeg / iZip / UnRarX for Mac
- 7-Zip / PeaZip for Linux

Downloading the color images of this book

We also provide you with a PDF file that has color images of the screenshots/diagrams used in this book. The color images will help you better understand the changes in the output. You can download this file from `http://www.packtpub.com/sites/default/files/downloads/CanvasCookbook_ColorImages.pdf`.

Errata

Although we have taken every care to ensure the accuracy of our content, mistakes do happen. If you find a mistake in one of our books—maybe a mistake in the text or the code—we would be grateful if you could report this to us. By doing so, you can save other readers from frustration and help us improve subsequent versions of this book. If you find any errata, please report them by visiting `http://www.packtpub.com/submit-errata`, selecting your book, clicking on the **Errata Submission Form** link, and entering the details of your errata. Once your errata are verified, your submission will be accepted and the errata will be uploaded to our website or added to any list of existing errata under the Errata section of that title.

To view the previously submitted errata, go to `https://www.packtpub.com/books/content/support` and enter the name of the book in the search field. The required information will appear under the **Errata** section.

Piracy

Piracy of copyrighted material on the Internet is an ongoing problem across all media. At Packt, we take the protection of our copyright and licenses very seriously. If you come across any illegal copies of our works in any form on the Internet, please provide us with the location address or website name immediately so that we can pursue a remedy.

Please contact us at `copyright@packtpub.com` with a link to the suspected pirated material.

We appreciate your help in protecting our authors and our ability to bring you valuable content.

Questions

If you have a problem with any aspect of this book, you can contact us at `questions@packtpub.com`, and we will do our best to address the problem.

1

Paths and Text

HTML5 Canvas is an element that provides the user with a workspace of a desired size for drawing. The Canvas API contains a rich set of drawing functions that can be accessed through **JavaScript**. The canvas element can be styled using **CSS** (**Cascaded Style Sheet**). CSS styling can improve performance and add interesting effects.

Thus, HTML5 Canvas programming can be done with the support of **JavaScript** and **CSS**.

Why HTML5 Canvas?

- ▶ HTML5 Canvas is fully *interactive*.
- ▶ Every object drawn on canvas can be *animated*.
- ▶ Canvas is *flexible* enough to let you draw dynamic graphics. Also it allows adding audio and video.
- ▶ All major *browsers support* canvas. However, the support and implementation differs from browser to browser.
- ▶ It is a *standard* open technology.
- ▶ Canvas is *portable*. Once created, an HTML5 Canvas application can run on almost all devices.
- ▶ To develop Canvas programs you just need a *code editor* and a *browser*. You can use sublime (available on www, Text, or HTMLPad), and you can test your code on Google Chrome or Firefox. You can find sublime text at `http://www.sublimetext.com/` and HTMLPad at `http://www.htmlpad.net/`. However, for the recipes in this book I have used Notepad.
- ▶ HTML5 Canvas can be used for gaming, advertising, data representation, *education and training,* and *art and decoration*.

Introduction

This chapter explains how to draw lines, arcs, curves, and text. These basic building blocks are further combined to create colorful and beautiful drawings. In this chapter we will cover:

- ▸ Drawing lines
- ▸ Drawing horizontal, vertical, and assorted lines
- ▸ Drawing joins
- ▸ Drawing arc1
- ▸ Drawing arc2
- ▸ Drawing a quadratic curve
- ▸ Drawing a rainbow
- ▸ Drawing a Bezier curve
- ▸ Drawing a flag
- ▸ Drawing text
- ▸ Drawing 3D text with shadows
- ▸ Adding shadows to objects
- ▸ Drawing a house

Drawing lines

The most basic shape in drawing is a line. Here you will see the various types of line that can be drawn. Also, you will see how different effects can be given to them.

This is the output of our first recipe:

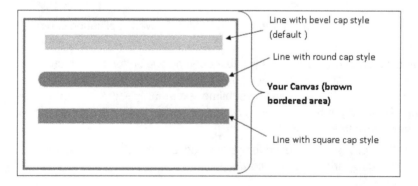

How to do it...

This recipe is made by undertaking the following steps:

1. Detect the canvas element.

2. Write the initiating function to create the canvas and its context.

3. Call the function to draw the line specified with different attributes.

The final code looks as follows:

```html
<html>
<head>
  <title>Simple Lines</title>
    <script type="text/javascript">
      var can;
      var ctx;
      function init() {
        can = document.getElementById("MyCanvasArea");
        ctx = can.getContext("2d");
        drawLine(30,30,300,30,20,"orange","butt");//default cap style
        drawLine(30,80,300,80,20,"crimson","round");
        drawLine(30,130,300,130,20,"teal","square");
      }
      function drawLine(xstart,ystart,xend,yend,width,color,cap)
      {
        ctx.beginPath();
        ctx.strokeStyle=color;
        ctx.lineWidth=width
        ctx.lineCap=cap;
        ctx.moveTo(xstart,ystart);
        ctx.lineTo(xend,yend);
        ctx.stroke();
        ctx.closePath();
      }
    </script>
</head>
<body onload="init()">
<br/><br/>
  <center>
    <canvas id="MyCanvasArea"
width="320"
height="200"
style="border:3px solid brown;">
```

```
Your browser doesn't support canvas
    </canvas>
  </center>
</body>
</html>
```

How it works...

To set up the canvas you need the canvas element, which is embedded in the body tag of the code. The Canvas created will be of 320 x 200 and will have a brown colored border. The border color and the dimensions are specified through the properties of the canvas element. If your browser doesn't support canvas then it will display **Your browser doesn't support canvas** as mentioned in the canvas element of the HTML code.

The `onload` property is responsible for invoking the `init()` function to initialize the canvas and context as soon as you run the program:

```
<body onload="init()">
<canvas id="MyCanvasArea"
width="320"
height="200"
style="border:2px solid brown;">
</body>
```

The `init()` function, which is a part of `<script>` tag, has two parts:

 ▸ Detecting the canvas
 ▸ Calling the relevant functions

The following snippet shows how to do it:

```
function init() {
    can = document.getElementById("MyCanvasArea");
    ctx = can.getContext("2d");
    drawLine(30,30,300,30,20,"orange","butt");  //default cap
    style
    drawLine(30,80,300,80,20,"crimson","round");
    drawLine(30,130,300,130,20,"teal","square");
}
```

The purpose of the canvas API functions used in the preceding snippet are briefed here:

- `getElementById()`: This function returns the element that has the ID attribute with the specified value. In our case the ID is **MyCanvasArea**. The function returns a null value if the ID doesn't exist. If there are two elements with the same ID then it returns the first element from the source code.

- `getContext()`: This function returns a 2D drawing context on the canvas. It returns a null value if it is not supported by the browser.

The next part of `init()` calls the `drawLine()` function to draw a line on the canvas. The parameters/arguments passed to the function are the two coordinates of the line to be drawn, the width, the color, and the cap style.

The following is the function definition:

```
function drawLine(xstart,ystart,xend,yend,width,color,cap)
{
  ctx.beginPath();
  ctx.strokeStyle=color;
  ctx.lineWidth=width;
  ctx.lineCap=cap;
  ctx.moveTo(xstart,ystart);
  ctx.lineTo(xend,yend);
  ctx.stroke();
  ctx.closePath();
}
```

The following functions of the canvas API are used in here:

- `beginPath()`: Starts a new path by emptying the list of sub-paths. It resets the current path. This function can be called whenever new paths need to be created.

- `moveTo(x,y)`: Moves the starting point of the new sub-path to the `(x,y)` coordinates. This is like placing your pencil at a particular point from where you want to start drawing.

- `lineTo(x,y)`: Connects the last point in the sub-path to the `(x,y)` coordinates with a straight line. This function actually doesn't draw the line, it just connects it.

- `stroke()`: Strokes the given path with the stroke style using the non-zero winding rule. This function actually draws the path.

- `closePath()`: This is the function to end a path.

The following properties of the canvas API are used here:

- `strokeStyle`: This defines the color in which the strokes are to be applied.
- `lineWidth`: This defines the thickness of the line.
- `lineCap`: This defines the cap style. There are three types, namely butt, round and square. The butt style is default. For round and square styles, extra length is added on both sides of the line. This is 1/2 of the width specified by you. You can see the difference in length of the first and last two lines shown in the output.

The cap style has an impact on the display. Notice the length of the first and the next two lines in the output. The next two lines have a longer length because of their cap styles.

The **butt** value means that no additional line cap is added.

The **round** value means that a semi-circle with the diameter equal to the `lineWidth` (in our example it is 20) is added on both sides.

The **square** value means that a rectangle of length the same as lineWidth and width the same as half of the lineWidth is added on both sides of the line.

The effects of butt and square look similar; however the lengths of lines differ.

You can create your own functions for common lines of code wherever you find it necessary. For example, the following two lines of code can be converted into a function that returns the canvas context:

```
can = document.getElementById("MyCanvasArea");
ctx = can.getContext("2d");
```

Also, depending on the return value of `getContext()`, you can detect whether your browser supports canvas.

There's more...

You can definitely try the following:

- Comment the lines that call `beginPath()` and `closePath()`
- Change the width and height of the canvas
- Try changing the colors to green, yellow, pink, magenta, and so on
- Call the `drawLine()` function with appropriate parameters to draw one more line

Drawing horizontal, vertical, and assorted lines

The output of our second recipe looks like this:

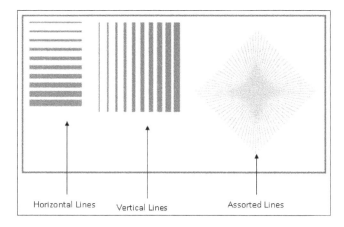

Horizontal Lines   Vertical Lines   Assorted Lines

How to do it...

A small change in the previous example builds our new recipe.

You need to do the following to build this recipe:

1. Add three different functions named `drawHorizontalLines()`, `drawVerticalLines()`, and `drawAssortedLines()` to the `<script>` tag.

2. Call these functions through the `init()` method, the same way as the `drawLine()` function was called.

After making the necessary changes, our recipe looks like this:

```
<html>
<head>
  <title>Lines Lines and More Lines</title>
    <script type="text/javascript">
      var can;
      var ctx;
      function init() {
        can = document.getElementById("MyCanvasArea");
        ctx = can.getContext("2d");
        drawHorizontalLines();
        drawVerticalLines();
```

```
        drawAssortedLines();
}
function drawLine(xstart,ystart,xend,yend,width,color)
{
  ctx.beginPath();
  ctx.strokeStyle=color;
  ctx.lineWidth=width;
  ctx.moveTo(xstart,ystart);
  ctx.lineTo(xend,yend);
  ctx.stroke();
  ctx.closePath();
}
function drawHorizontalLines()
{
  xs=10;   ys=10;xe=100; ye=10;
  c="teal"; w=2;
  //draw 10 lines
  for(i=1;i<=10;i++)
  {
    drawLine(xs,ys,xe,ye,w++,c);
    ys+=15;   //change through y axis
    ye+=15;
  }
}
function drawVerticalLines()
{
  xs=130;   ys=10;xe=130;ye=160;
  c="crimson";w=2;
  //draw 10 lines
  for(i=1;i<=10;i++)
  {
    drawLine(xs,ys,xe,ye,w++,c);
    xs+=15; //change through x axis
    xe+=15;
  }
}
function drawAssortedLines()
{
  //center point
  xcenter=400;ycenter=125;   xe=xcenter-100;ye=ycenter;
  c="orange";   w=2;
  //Second quadrant
  for(xe=xcenter-100;xe<=xcenter;xe+=5,ye-=5)
    drawLine(xcenter,ycenter,xe,ye,w,c);
```

```
            //first quadrant
            for(ye=ycenter-100;ye<=ycenter;xe+=5,ye+=5)
              drawLine(xcenter,ycenter,xe,ye,w,c);
            //fourth quadrant
            for(xe=xcenter+100;xe>=xcenter;xe-=5,ye+=5)
              drawLine(xcenter,ycenter,xe,ye,w,c);
            //third quadrant
            for(ye=ycenter+100;ye>=ycenter;xe-=5,ye-=5)
              drawLine(xcenter,ycenter,xe,ye,w,c);
          }
      </script>
  </head>
  <body onload="init()">
    <br/><br/>
    <center>
    <canvas id="MyCanvasArea" height="260" width="520" style="border:3px
solid brown;">
    </canvas>
    </center>
  </body>
</html>
```

For convenience, the function names and their calls shown through `init()` are made in bold to help you to understand where to make changes in the previous recipe.

How it works...

The basic functions `moveTo()` and `lineTo()` remain the same. However, three different functions are created, which contain loops to repeatedly call the previously mentioned line drawing function.

In the `drawHorizontalLines()`,the lines are drawn along the *x* axis. In each iteration, the width of the line increases, thereby showing a gradual increase in thickness.

In the `drawVerticalLines()` function, the lines are drawn along the *y* axis.

The function `drawAssortedLines()` has four different loops drawing lines in four different quadrants. The `drawLine()` function is used in the loop and, in every iteration, the parameter values for the function change to draw lines starting from different coordinates. For instance, in the first loop, the value of `xe` starts from `300`, which is less than the value of `xcenter`. So, we start drawing from the left side of the center. On every iteration, the value of `xe` increases and the value for `ye` decreases by `5`. Thus, the starting point of a line moves a bit inwards and a bit upwards. The line is drawn from (`xe`,`ye`) to (`xcenter`,`ycenter`). The quadrants are filled in, in an anticlockwise direction, starting from the 2nd quadrant.

When you apply the concept of quadrants, bear in mind that the center is (400,125) and not (0,0).

All three functions mentioned previously are called within init().

There's more...

Try the following:

- Change the order in which the functions are called
- Increase the number in the terminating condition of the loop from 10 to some higher number
- Change the colors

Drawing joins

This topic focuses on the lineJoin property of the context object.

The lineJoin property allows you to join two lines with three different effects. They are:

- bevel (default)
- round
- miter

The effect of lineJoin can be easily observed in the output of our new recipe:

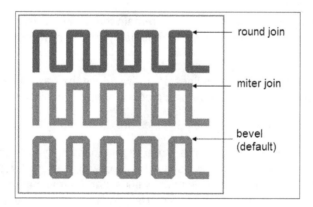

How to do it...

Again a small change in our first recipe makes this recipe.

Replace the `drawLine()` function with `drawJoinedLines()` and then call this function (three times) from `init()`.

The recipe looks like this:

```
<html>
<head>
  <title>Simple Canvas</title>
    <script type="text/javascript">
      var can;
      var ctx;
      function init() {
        can = document.getElementById("MyCanvasArea");
        ctx = can.getContext("2d");
        drawJoinedLines(50,150,50,50,20,"blue","round");
        drawJoinedLines(50,300,50,200,20,"red","miter");
        drawJoinedLines(50,450,50,350,20,"green","bevel");
      }
      function drawJoinedLines(xstart,ystart,xnext,ynext,width,color,
      jointype){
        ctx.beginPath();
        ctx.lineJoin=jointype;
        ctx.lineCap="square";
        ctx.strokeStyle=color;
        ctx.lineWidth=width;
        x1=xstart;  y1=ystart;  x2=xnext;  y2=ynext;
        ctx.moveTo(x1,y1);
        for(i=1;i<=20;i+=1){
          ctx.lineTo(x2,y2);
          if(i%2==1){    //if 1 line is drawn, move along x axis
            x2=x2+50;
          }
          else{
            if(y2>ynext)
              y2=ynext;
            else
              y2=y2+100;
          }
        }
        ctx.stroke();
        ctx.closePath();
```

```
        }
    </script>
</head>
<body onload="init()">
    <br/><br/>
    <center>
    <canvas id="MyCanvasArea" height="500" width="600" style="border:3px
    solid brown;">
    </canvas>
    </center>
</body>
</html>
```

How it works...

Here, the main function, which does the job for us, is `drawJoinedLines()`. This function is called through the `init()` function three times. Obviously the output shows three different ways in which the lines are joined.

Outside the `for` loop we move to the `(x1,y1)` coordinates to start the drawing. The function `lineTo()` mentioned in the loop draws a line between `(x1,y1)` and `(x2,y2)`. In the first iteration, the vertical line is drawn and the end points for the next line are set. If the line to be drawn is horizontal, we increment the value of `x2` by `50`, thus moving along the *x* axis. If the line to be drawn is vertical, then we increment the value of the *y* coordinate by `100` moving vertically downwards. The loop executes 20 times, drawing `10` vertical and `10` horizontal lines.

The function `drawJoinedLines()` is called three times from `init()`, each time specifying the different start point and join type. The effect of the joins can be seen in the output.

Drawing arc1

There are two different functions that allow drawing an arc. One of the functions is `arcTo(xctrl,yctrl,xPos,yPos,radius)`.

You will see the second function in the next recipe. The arcTo() function accepts two coordinates and a radius. To use the `arcTo()` function work, it is necessary to first mark the position from where the arc is to be drawn. This is done by calling the `moveTo()` function, the same way as we do for drawing a line (refer to the `lineTo()` function).

The output of our arc recipe is as follows:

How to do it...

The recipe is as follows:

```
<html>
<head>
<title>Basic Arc</title>
<script>
  function init()
  {
  can = document.getElementById("MyCanvasArea");
  ctx = can.getContext("2d");

    drawArcMethod1(60,150,100,80,140,150,25,"blue");

    //function to draw curve by method 1
    function drawArcMethod1(xPos,yPos,xctrl,yctrl,xend,yend,radius,li
necolor)
    {
      ctx.strokeStyle = linecolor;
      ctx.fillStyle="red";
      ctx.lineWidth    = 8;

      ctx.beginPath();
      ctx.moveTo(xPos,yPos);
      ctx.arcTo(xctrl,yctrl,xend,yend,radius);
      //ctx.fill();
      ctx.stroke();
    }
  }
```

```
</script>
</head>
<body onload="init()">
<canvas ID="MyCanvasArea" width="300" height="300" style="border:2px
solid black;">
  your browser doesn't support canvas
</canvas>
</body>
</html>
```

How it works...

In our recipe, the syntax to draw the arc is as follows:

```
ctx.moveTo(xPos,yPos);
ctx.arcTo(xctrl,yctrl,xend,yend,radius);
```

On the canvas, the arc is drawn by following these steps:

1. Move to a coordinate (xPos,yPos).

2. Draw an imaginary line between (xPos,yPos) and the control point (xctrl,yctrl).

3. Then draw an imaginary line between (xctrl,yctrl) and the end coordinate (xend,yend), thereby generating a cone shape.

4. Draw an imaginary circle with the given radius between the two mentioned lines in such a way that the two lines are tangents to the circle at two different points.

5. The arc is the path drawn between these two tangent points.

Here is a diagrammatic representation:

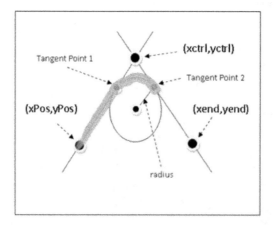

The arc as shown previously will appear for the following parameters:

```
xPos,yPos = (60,150)
xctrl,yctrl=(100,80)
xend,yend=(140,150)
radius=15
```

If you increase the radius of the circle, the size will increase but it will lie within the angle formed by the two lines intersecting at the control point (xctrl,yctrl). So the circle will shift downwards, forming two tangent points, and the arc will bend. It will look as follows if the radius is increased to 25:

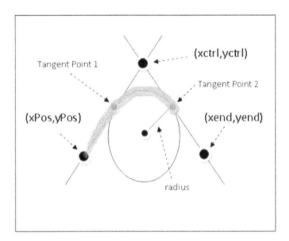

There's more...

Try the following in the recipe:

- ► Change the color of the arc
- ► Increase the radius
- ► Draw multiple arcs

Drawing arc2

The second function, arc(xPos,yPos,radius,startAngle,endAngle,anticlockwise), is much easier and is used to develop our new recipe. The parameters here mean the following:

- ► xPos: The x coordinate of the arc's center.
- ► yPos: The y coordinate of the arc's center.
- ► radius: The arc's radius.

- ▶ `startAngle`: The angle at which the arc starts, measured clockwise from the positive *x* axis and expressed in **radians**.

- ▶ `endAngle`: The angle at which the arc ends, measured clockwise from the positive *x* axis and expressed in radians.

- ▶ `Anticlockwise` (optional): A Boolean value which, if `True`, causes the arc to be drawn counter-clockwise between the two angles. By default the arc is drawn clockwise.

Two new things are introduced here:

- ▶ The `fillStyle` property, which decides the color with which the arc needs to be filled

- ▶ The `fill()` method, which actually fills the area of the arc that you draw

The output of this recipe looks like this:

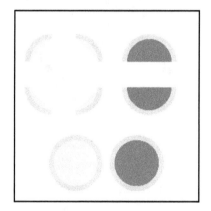

How to do it...

Here is the recipe:

```
<html>
<head>
<title>Arcs</title>
<script>
  function init()
  {
  can = document.getElementById("MyCanvasArea");
  ctx = can.getContext("2d");
```

```
drawArc(60,80,40,180,270,false,"aqua","yellow");
drawArc(120,80,40,270,360,false,"aqua","yellow");
drawArc(220,80,40,180,360,false,"aqua","red");

drawArc(60,150,40,90,180,false,"aqua","yellow");
drawArc(120,150,40,0,90,false,"aqua","yellow");
drawArc(220,150,40,0,180,false,"aqua","red");

drawArc(100,250,40,0,360,false,"aqua","yellow");
drawArc(200,250,40,360,0,false,"aqua","red");

//function to draw curve
function drawArc(xPos,yPos,radius,startAngle,endAngle,
anticlockwise,lineColor, fillColor,width)
    {
        var startAngle = startAngle * (Math.PI/180);
        var endAngle   = endAngle   * (Math.PI/180);

        var radius = radius;

        ctx.strokeStyle = lineColor;
        ctx.fillStyle   = fillColor;
        ctx.lineWidth   = width;

        ctx.beginPath();
        ctx.arc(xPos,yPos,radius,startAngle,endAngle,anticlockwise);

        ctx.fill();
        ctx.stroke();
    }
}
</script>
</head>
<body onload="init()">
<canvas ID="MyCanvasArea" width="300" height="300" style="border:2px
solid black;">
  your browser doesn't support canvas
</canvas>
</body>
</html>
```

How it works...

Consider the following diagram for an explanation:

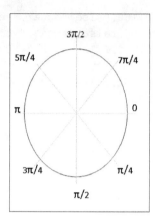

The arc function accepts the angles in radians. Refer to the circle shown previously for a better understanding. If you specify the start angle as zero and end angle as π, then you should see a semicircle drawn in a clockwise direction (starting from zero through π/2 and ending on π). If you are comfortable with angles in degrees then they need to be converted into radians before passing into the function. The formula for conversion is:
*Value in Radians = value in degrees * (π/180).*

A partial chart of conversion is shown as follows:

Angle in degrees	Angle in radians
0	0
30	π/6
45	π/4
60	π/3
.	.
.	.
.	.

There's more...

Try the following:

- ▸ Comment the statements `usesfillStyle` and `fillColor`
- ▸ Change the value for `fillStyle`
- ▸ Change the angles

Drawing a quadratic curve

In this recipe, you will learn how to draw a quadratic curve. The quadratic curve provides much more flexibility. These curves can be used to create custom shapes in numerous drawings. You will find one implementation in the next recipe:

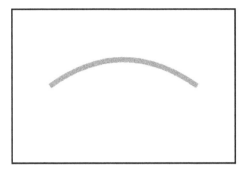

How to do it...

Here is a simple code to draw a quadratic curve:

```
<html>
  <head>
    <title>Arcs</title>
    <script>
    function init()
    {
      can  = document.getElementById("MyCanvasArea");
      ctx = can.getContext("2d");

      //call to the function to draw curve
      drawQuadraticCurve(50,100,150,30,250,100,'#df34ef',7);

      //function to draw quadratic curve
      function drawQuadraticCurve(xStart,yStart,xControl, yControl,
      xEnd, yEnd,color,width)
      {
        ctx.beginPath();
        ctx.strokeStyle=color;
        ctx.lineJoin="round";
        ctx.lineWidth=width;
        ctx.moveTo(xStart,yStart);
```

```
        ctx.quadraticCurveTo(xControl, yControl, xEnd, yEnd);
        ctx.stroke();
        ctx.closePath();
    }
}
</script>
</head>
<body onload="init()">
<canvas ID="MyCanvasArea" width="300" height="200"
style="border:2px solid black;">
your browser doesn't support canvas
</canvas>
</body>
</html>
```

How it works...

The API function is quadraticCurveTo(cpX, cpY, epX, epY).

In this function, cpX and cpY are coordinates of the control point, and epX and epY are coordinates of the end point, the drawing has to start from some point. However, it is not part of this function. You have to move to a point that you want to draw from. This is done by using the moveTo() function.

Refer to the diagram:

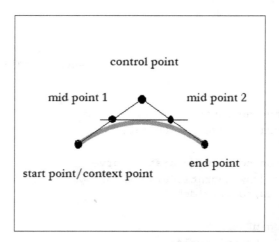

Observe the points in the diagram. The parameters passed to the quadraticCurveTo() function are coordinates of the control point and end point. Before this function is called you need to call a function moveTo() from where you specify the start/context point.

There's more...

Try the following:

▸ Change the control point to `(150,150)`

▸ Change the other coordinates and observe the output

Drawing a rainbow

This is an implementation of a quadratic curve.

The output of our new recipe looks like this:

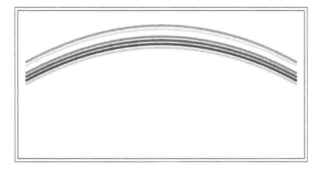

How to do it...

The recipe is quite simple, comprising seven calls to the function `quadraticTo()` to draw seven different curves.

Here is the recipe:

```html
<html>
<head>
  <title>Rainbow</title>
  <script type="text/javascript">
    var can;
    var ctx;
    function init() {
      can = document.getElementById("MyCanvasArea");
      ctx = can.getContext("2d");
      y=can.height/2;
      x=can.width-20;
      mid=can.width/2;
      //rainbow - vibgyor
```

```
        drawQuadraticCurve(20,y,mid,0,x,y,"violet",7);
        drawQuadraticCurve(20,y-10,mid,-10,x,y-10,"indigo",7);
        drawQuadraticCurve(20,y-20,mid,-20,x,y-20,"blue",7);
        drawQuadraticCurve(20,y-30,mid,-30,x,y-30,"green",7);
        drawQuadraticCurve(20,y-40,mid,-40,x,y-40,"yellow",7);
        drawQuadraticCurve(20,y-50,mid,-50,x,y-50,"orange",7);
        drawQuadraticCurve(20,y-60,mid,-60,x,y-60,"red",7);


    }
    function drawQuadraticCurve(xStart,yStart,xControl, yControl,
    xEnd, yEnd,color,width)
    {
        //refer the previous recipe for code
        //....
    }
  </script>
</head>
<body onload="init()">
  <canvas id="MyCanvasArea" width="800" height="400" style="border:2px
  solid black;" >
    browser doesn't support canvas
  </canvas>
</body>
</html>
```

How it works...

The `drawQuadraticCurveTo()` is the same function as used in the previous recipe. This function is called multiple times from the `init()` method.

Drawing a Bezier curve

A Bezier curve is different from a quadratic curve. It is also known as a cubic curve and is the most advanced curvature available in HTML5. The simple Bezier curve looks as shown in the output of this recipe:

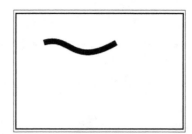

How to do it...

The recipe is as follows:

```html
<html>

<head>

<title>A Bezier Curve</title>
<script>
  function init()
  {
    can  = document.getElementById("MyCanvasArea");
    ctx = can.getContext("2d");
    var xstart = 50;    var ystart = 50;
    var xctrl1 = 100;   var yctrl1 = 35;
    var xctrl2 = 100;   var yctrl2 = 95;
    var xend = 180;   var yend = ystart;
    //call to the function
    drawBezierCurve(xstart,ystart,xctrl1,yctrl1,xctrl2,yctrl2,xend,
    yend,"black",10);
  }
  function drawBezierCurve(xstart,ystart,xctrl1,yctrl1,xctrl2,yctrl2,
  xend,yend,color,width)

  {

    ctx.strokeStyle=color;

    ctx.lineWidth=width;
    ctx.beginPath();
    ctx.moveTo(xstart,ystart);
    ctx.bezierCurveTo(xctrl1,yctrl1,xctrl2,yctrl2,xend,yend);
    ctx.stroke();
  }
</script>
</head>
<body onload="init()">

  <canvas id="MyCanvasArea" width ="300"  height="200"
  style="border:2px solid black">

    Your browser doesn't currently support HTML5 Canvas.

  </canvas>
</body>
</html>
```

How it works...

In a Bezier curve there are two control points, one start point and one end point. So you have to move to the starting or context point, like we do in a quadratic curve, and then specify the control points and ending point in the `bezierCurveTo(cp1X, cp1Y, cp2X, cp2Y, epX, epY)` method. Here, `cp1` and `cp2` are the control points and `ep` is the end point. The two control points add more flexibility to the curve.

Refer to the diagram given here:

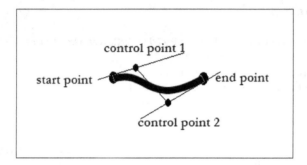

The curve starts at the start/context point and ends at the end point. It heads towards control point 1 and then comes down to the end point through control point 2. The control points control the curvature. Change the *y* coordinate of any control point and you will see the difference.

Bezier curves are actually a sequence of cubic segments rather than linear segments. They appear smooth at all scales and are used in computer graphics.

Drawing a flag

Using the knowledge of Bezier curves you can develop various examples of your own. Here is a recipe whose output looks like this:

How to do it...

If you observe the drawing of a flag, you can easily understand that it's drawn using a combination of a line, a Bezier curve, and a circle. Here is our recipe:

```html
<html>
<head>
<title>A Flag</title>
<script>
  function init()
  {
    can = document.getElementById("MyCanvasArea");
    ctx = can.getContext("2d");
    var xstart = 50;    var ystart = 25;
    var xctrl1 = 100;   var yctrl1 = 10;
    var xctrl2 = 100;   var yctrl2 = 70;
    var xend = 180;   var yend = ystart;

    //10 curves having orange color
    for(i=1;i<=10;i++)
    {
      drawBezierCurve(xstart,ystart,xctrl1,yctrl1,xctrl2,yctrl2,xend,
      yend,"orange");
      ystart+=5;yend+=5;yctrl1+=5;yctrl2+=5;
    }
    //10 curves having white color
    for(j=1;j<=10;j++)
    {
      drawBezierCurve(xstart,ystart,xctrl1,yctrl1,xctrl2,yctrl2,xend,
      yend,"white");
      ystart+=5;yend+=5;yctrl1+=5;yctrl2+=5;
    }
    //10 curves having green color
    for(j=1;j<=10;j++)
    {
      drawBezierCurve(xstart,ystart,xctrl1,yctrl1,xctrl2,yctrl2,xend,
      yend,"green");
      ystart+=5;yend+=5;yctrl1+=5;yctrl2+=5;
    }
    //the ashoka wheel we draw two arcs and lines
    x1=120;
    y1=113;
    drawArc(x1,y1,22,0,360,false,"navy");
    //draw a stand for the flag
```

```
        drawLine(50,350,50,20,10,"brown");
    }
function drawBezierCurve(xstart,ystart,xctrl1,yctrl1,xctrl2,yctrl2,
xend,yend,color,width)
{
    ctx.strokeStyle=color;
    ctx.lineWidth=6;
    ctx.beginPath();
    ctx.moveTo(xstart,ystart);
    ctx.bezierCurveTo(xctrl1,yctrl1,xctrl2,yctrl2,xend,yend);
    ctx.stroke();
}
function drawArc(xPos,yPos,radius,startAngle,endAngle,
anticlockwise,lineColor)
{
    var startAngle = startAngle * (Math.PI/180);
    var endAngle   = endAngle   * (Math.PI/180);
    var radius = radius;
    ctx.strokeStyle = lineColor;
    ctx.fillStyle="navy";
    ctx.lineWidth   = 4;
    ctx.beginPath();
    ctx.arc(xPos,yPos,radius,startAngle,endAngle,anticlockwise);
    ctx.fill();
    ctx.stroke();
}
function drawLine(xstart,ystart,xend,yend,width,color)
{
    ctx.beginPath();
    ctx.strokeStyle=color;
    ctx.lineWidth=width;
    ctx.moveTo(xstart,ystart);
    ctx.lineTo(xend,yend);
    ctx.stroke();
    ctx.closePath();
}
</script>
</head>
<body onload="init()">
  <canvas id="MyCanvasArea" width ="300"  height="400"
  style="border:2px solid black">
    Your browser doesn't currently support HTML5 Canvas.
  </canvas>
</body>
</html>
```

How it works...

In the recipe, you will notice that the function to draw a Bezier curve is called 10 times through a loop for different coordinates and colors. Other than this, a vertical line with a thickness of 10 is drawn. For this, the function `drawLine()` is called specifying the appropriate parameters.

Drawing text

This is a simple recipe rendering text:

How to do it...

The recipe is as follows:

```
<html>

<head>

<title>A Simple Text</title>
<script>
  function init()
  {
    can  = document.getElementById("MyCanvasArea");

    ctx = can.getContext("2d");

    var X=Math.round(can.width/2);

    drawLine(X,10,X,390,2,'black','butt');

    drawMyText(X,50,'Sujata-An Architect & an Entrepreneur','center',
    'top','blue');
```

```
        drawMyText(X,100,'Prashant-An MBA','left','middle','green');
        drawMyText(X,150,'Amit-An Engineer','right','bottom','red');
        drawMyText(X,200,'Sampada-An Engineer','start','alphabetic',
        'orange');
        drawMyText(X,250,'Sukhada-A Classical Singer','end','hanging',
        'aqua');
        drawMyText(X,300,'Kalyani-A Chartered Accountant','center',
        'ideographic','magenta');
        ctx.direction="rtl";
        drawMyText(X,350,'Vivek-An IITian','start','alphabetic','navy');
    }
    function drawMyText(X,Y,message,align,baseline,color)
    {

        ctx.beginPath();
        ctx.fillStyle=color;
        ctx.font='20pt Arial';

        ctx.textAlign=align;
        ctx.textBaseLine=baseline;
        ctx.fillText(message,X,Y);
        ctx.closePath();
    }
    function drawLine(xstart,ystart,xend,yend,width,color,cap)
    {
        ctx.beginPath();
        ctx.strokeStyle=color;
        ctx.lineWidth=width;
        ctx.lineCap=cap;
        ctx.moveTo(xstart,ystart);
        ctx.lineTo(xend,yend);
        ctx.stroke();
        ctx.closePath();
    }
</script>
</head>
<body onload="init()">

  <canvas id="MyCanvasArea" width ="800"  height="400"
  style="border:2px solid black">

    Your browser doesn't currently support HTML5 Canvas.

  </canvas>
</body>
</html>
```

How it works...

The output demonstrates the `textAlign` property. The values for this property can be `left`, `right`, `center`, `start`, or `end`. The value `start` is the same as `left` if the direction of text is from left to right, and the text display starts from the coordinates specified. In this recipe, it starts from `400,100` and `400,200` for two different texts. Observe the last text. The text seems to end on the line; however, the property is set with the value `start`. This happens because of this statement:

```
ctx.direction="rtl";
```

The direction of text rendered on the canvas is changed from default to right-to-left, so the start of the text changes. By default the direction is inherited from the parent element. Otherwise, it can be set to left-to-right or right-to-left.

There's more...

Use the `strokeText()` method instead of `fillText()`. You will need to replace `fillStyle()` with `strokeStyle()`.

Drawing 3D text with shadows

If 2D text doesn't get you jazzed, you might consider drawing 3D text instead. Although the HTML5 canvas API doesn't directly provide us with a means of creating 3D text, we can certainly create a custom `draw3dText()` method using the existing API:

How to do it...

The recipe is as follows:

```html
<html>
<head>

<title>A 3D Text</title>
<script>
  function init()
  {
    can  = document.getElementById("MyCanvasArea");

    ctx = can.getContext("2d");

    var X=Math.round(can.width/2);

    drawLine(X,10,X,390,2,'black','butt');

    draw3dText(X,50,'Sujata-An Architect & an Entrepreneur','center',
    'top','blue',1);
    draw3dText(X,100,'Prashant-An MBA','left','middle','green',2);
    draw3dText(X,150,'Amit-An Engineer','right','bottom','red',3);
    draw3dText(X,200,'Sampada-An Engineer','start','alphabetic',
    'orange',4);
    draw3dText(X,250,'Sukhada-A Classical Singer','end','hanging',
    'aqua',5);
    draw3dText(X,300,'Kalyani-A Chartered Accountant','center',
    'ideographic','magenta',6);
    ctx.direction="rtl";
    draw3dText(X,350,'Vivek-An IITian','start','alphabetic','navy',7);
  }
  function draw3dText(X,Y,message,align,baseline,color,depth)

  {

    ctx.beginPath();
    var i=0;
    ctx.font='20pt Arial';

    ctx.textAlign=align;
    ctx.textBaseLine=baseline;
    ctx.fillStyle=color;
    ctx.fillText(message,X,Y);
```

```
        ctx.shadowColor="lightgrey";
        ctx.shadowBlur=5;
        while(i<=depth)
        {
            ctx.shadowOffsetX=depth+1;
            ctx.shadowOffsetY=depth+2;
            ctx.fillText(message,X,Y);
            i++;
        }
        ctx.closePath();
    }
    function drawLine(xstart,ystart,xend,yend,width,color,cap)
    {
    //refer the first recipe
    //....
    }
</script>
</head>
<body onload="init()">
    <canvas id="MyCanvasArea" width ="800"  height="400"
    style="border:2px solid black">

            Your browser doesn't currently support HTML5 Canvas.

    </canvas>
</body>
</html>
```

How it works...

This recipe is created by appending some code to the function for drawing the text. The properties to apply shadow are used on the text. The properties shadowColor, shadowOffsetX, shadowOffsetY, and shadowBlur are set to achieve the 3D effect. Before the loop begins, the text is drawn with the specified color. Then the shadow color and blur level is set. And within the loop, the text is drawn with changed X and Y offset for the shadow for certain depth. The properties used are summarized here:

Property	Description
shadowOffsetY	Sets or returns the vertical distance of the shadow from the shape.
shadowOffsetX	Sets or returns the horizontal distance of the shadow from the shape.
shadowBlur	Sets or returns the blur level for shadows.
shadowColor	Sets or returns the color to use for shadows.

There's more...

Try the following:

- Changing the color of the shadow
- Increasing the depth

Adding shadows to objects

Here, we will be using our first recipe. Just a few properties are set and we get a different output as shown:

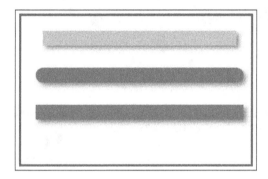

Notice the difference between this and the output of the first recipe. Here you will notice a shadow for each line.

How to do it...

We use a few shadow-related properties to build this recipe:

```
<html>
<head>
  <title>Line Shadow</title>
    <script type="text/javascript">
      var can;
      var ctx;
      function init() {
        can = document.getElementById("MyCanvasArea");
        ctx = can.getContext("2d");
        drawLine(30,30,300,30,20,"orange","butt");  //default cap
        style
        drawLine(30,80,300,80,20,"crimson","round");
        drawLine(30,130,300,130,20,"teal","square");
```

```
        }
      function drawLine(xstart,ystart,xend,yend,width,color,cap)
      {
        ctx.beginPath();
        ctx.strokeStyle=color;
        ctx.lineWidth=width;

        //adding shadow
        ctx.shadowOffsetX = 4;
        ctx.shadowOffsetY = 4;
        ctx.shadowBlur    = 7;
        ctx.shadowColor   = "gray";
        //shadow properties set above

        ctx.lineCap=cap;
        ctx.moveTo(xstart,ystart);
        ctx.lineTo(xend,yend);
        ctx.stroke();
        ctx.closePath();
      }
    </script>
</head>
<body onload="init()">
  <br/><br/>
  <center>
  <canvas id="MyCanvasArea" width="320" height="200"
  style="border:3px solid brown;">
  </canvas>
  </center>
</body>
</html>
```

How it works...

The properties related to the shadow mentioned in the previous recipe are used here. Here the shadow is applied to the line rather than the text. Thus, shadows can be applied to objects.

There's more...

Try the following:

- Change the shadow color
- Change the blur value for the shadow
- Change the shadowOffsetX and shadowOffsetY value

Drawing a house

The final recipe of the chapter combines all the building blocks learned so far. Here is the output of our first drawing. As a kid, everyone loves to draw this:

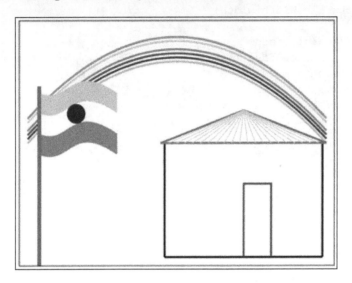

How to do it...

The recipe is just a combination of all the different functions developed and used so far. Here is the recipe:

```
<html>
<head>
  <title>My House</title>
    <script type="text/javascript">
      var can;
      var ctx;
      function init() {

        can = document.getElementById("myhouse");
        ctx = can.getContext("2d");
        drawRainbow();
        drawHouse();
        drawFlag();

      }
      function drawLine(xstart,ystart,xend,yend,width,color)
      {
```

```
    ctx.beginPath();
    ctx.lineJoin="miter";
    ctx.strokeStyle=color;
    ctx.lineWidth=width;
    ctx.moveTo(xstart,ystart);
    ctx.lineTo(xend,yend);
    ctx.stroke();
    ctx.closePath();
}
function drawHouse()
{

  x1=can.width/2-30;
  y1=can.height-20;
  x2=can.width-30;
  y2=can.height-20;
  color="black";
  width=5;
  drawLine(x1,y1,x2,y2,width,color);    //base
  drawLine(x1,y1,x1,can.height/2,width,color);  //left wall
  drawLine(x2,y2,x2,can.height/2,width,color);  //right wall

  x3=x1-10;
  y3=can.height/2;
  x4=x2+10;
  y4=can.height/2;
  drawLine(x3,y3,x4,y4,width,"brown");     //roof base

  x5=x1+(x2-x1)/2;           //midpoint of the roof
  y5=can.height/2-80;

  drawLine(x3,y3,x5,y5,width,"brown");    //roof - left side
  drawLine(x4,y4,x5,y5,width,"brown");    //roof - right side
  //rslope=(x5-x4)/(y5-y4);
  j=20;
  k=23;
  g=1;
  m=4;
  for(i=1;i<=20;i++)
  {
    var X1=x3+j;
    var Y1=y3;
    var X2=x5;
    var Y2=y5;
```

```
        drawLine(var X1,var Y1,var X2,var Y2,2,"orange");
        j=j+20;
        k=k+23;
    }
    //draw the door
    dX1=x1+(x5-x1);
    dY1=y1;
    dX2=x5;
    dY2=y5+180;
    ctx.beginPath();
    ctx.strokeStyle="blue";
    ctx.lineWidth=5;
    ctx.lineJoin="miter";
    ctx.moveTo(dX1,dY1);
    ctx.lineTo(dX2,dY2);
    ctx.lineTo(dX2+70,dY2);
    ctx.lineTo(dX1+70,dY1);
    ctx.stroke();
}
function drawRainbow()
{
    y=can.height/2;
    x=can.width-20;
    mid=can.width/2;
    //rainbow - vibgyor
    yc=-100;
    drawQuadraticCurve(20,y,mid,yc,x,y,"violet");
    drawQuadraticCurve(20,y-10,mid,yc-10,x,y-10,"indigo");
    drawQuadraticCurve(20,y-20,mid,yc-20,x,y-20,"blue");
    drawQuadraticCurve(20,y-30,mid,yc-30,x,y-30,"green");
    drawQuadraticCurve(20,y-40,mid,yc-40,x,y-40,"yellow");
    drawQuadraticCurve(20,y-50,mid,yc-50,x,y-50,"orange");
    drawQuadraticCurve(20,y-60,mid,yc-60,x,y-60,"red");
}
function drawFlag()
{
    var xstart = 50;    var ystart = 180;
    var xctrl1 = 130;   var yctrl1 = 210;
    var xctrl2 = 130;   var yctrl2 = 100;
    var xend = 250;   var yend = ystart;

    //10 curves having orange color
    for(i=1;i<=10;i++)
    {
```

```
    drawBezierCurve(xstart,ystart,xctrl1,yctrl1,xctrl2,yctrl2,
    xend,yend,"orange",6);
    ystart+=5;yend+=5;yctrl1+=5;yctrl2+=5;
  }
  //10 curves having white color
  for(j=1;j<=10;j++)
  {
    drawBezierCurve(xstart,ystart,xctrl1,yctrl1,xctrl2,yctrl2,
    xend,yend,"white",6);
    ystart+=5;yend+=5;yctrl1+=5;yctrl2+=5;
  }
  //10 curves having green color
  for(j=1;j<=10;j++)
  {
    drawBezierCurve(xstart,ystart,xctrl1,yctrl1,xctrl2,yctrl2,
    xend,yend,"green",6);
    ystart+=5;yend+=5;yctrl1+=5;yctrl2+=5;
  }

  x1=145;
  y1=228;
  drawArc(x1,y1,22,0,360,false,"black","navy");
  //draw a stand for the flag
  drawLine(50,650,50,160,10,"brown");
}
function drawQuadraticCurve(xstart,ystart,xControl, yControl,
xEnd, yEnd,color,width)
{
  //refer the Quadratic curve recipe
  //....
}
function drawBezierCurve(xstart,ystart,xctrl1,yctrl1,xctrl2,
yctrl2,xend,yend,color,width)

{

  //refer the Bezier curve recipe
  //....

}
function drawArc(xPos,yPos,radius,startAngle,endAngle,
anticlockwise,lineColor,fillColor,width)
 {
  //refer the Arc recipe
```

```
        //....
        }
    </script>
</head>
<body onload="init()">
  <canvas id="myhouse" height="600" width="800" style="border:2px
  solid black;">
  </canvas>
</body>
</html>
```

How it works...

The recipe is built on the concepts learned in the previous recipes. You will see here the use of a line, an arc, a quadratic curve, and a Bezier curve. All of these drawings are the building blocks for this recipe of a house. The functions are the same as used in the previous recipes. These functions are called to create a flag, a rainbow, and a hut, using only lines, arcs, and curves. Shapes can make your job easier. The next chapter is all about shapes.

2

Shapes and Composites

This chapter explains to draw various shapes. These basic building blocks are further combined to create desired drawings. In this chapter we will cover:

- ▶ Drawing rectangles
- ▶ Drawing triangles
- ▶ Drawing circles
- ▶ Drawing gradients
- ▶ Working with custom shapes and styles
- ▶ Demonstrating translation, rotation, and scaling
- ▶ Drawing an ellipse
- ▶ Saving and restoring canvas state
- ▶ Demonstrating compositions
- ▶ Drawing a mouse

Introduction

In this chapter, we will learn how to draw rectangles, triangles, circles, ellipses, and custom shapes. Also, we will learn to fill gradients, translation, rotation, and scaling to be applied on these shapes.

The recipe structure will be a bit different in this chapter. We will have the JavaScript code in a separate file and this file will be embedded in the HTML code at run-time. In the previous chapter, the complete recipe was in a single file (`.html` file). However, in this chapter, a single recipe will comprise two different files:

- ▶ An HTML file
- ▶ A JavaScript file

Also, the `can` (canvas) and `ctx` (context) objects are created within the `init()` function and the reference to `ctx` (context) is passed to the different functions called within `init()`.

Drawing rectangles

There are three different functions in the canvas API to draw rectangles. They are:

- `rect(xPos,yPos,width,height)`
- `fillRect(xPos,yPos,width,height)`
- `strokeRect(xPos,yPos,width,height)`

Let's see these all together in a single recipe. So here is the output of our first recipe:

Rectangles

How to do it...

The output that shows three different rectangles, uses a call to three different functions, which are explained further. The recipe is as follows.

An HTML file that includes the canvas element:

```
<html>
<head>
<title>Rectangles</title>
<script src="Rectangles.js"></script>
</head>
<body onload="init()" bgcolor="#FFFFCC">
<canvas id="canvas" width="250" height="200" style="border:2px solid
blue;" >
  your browser does not support canvas
</canvas>
<H1>Rectangles</H1>
</body>
</html>
```

The JavaScript file as mentioned in the `<script>` tag in the previously given code:

```
function init()
{
  var canvas = document.getElementById("canvas");
  if(canvas.getContext)
  {
    // Color of drawing, fillStyle is this color
    var ctx = canvas.getContext("2d");

    // Draw a square(rectangle with same sides)
    // from top left corner x,y, width, height
    ctx.strokeStyle="purple"
    ctx.rect(10,10,70,50);
    ctx.fillStyle="lightgreen";
    ctx.fill();
    ctx.stroke();

    //draw another rectangle
    ctx.fillStyle="crimson";
    ctx.fillRect (50,25, 100,100);

    //draw yet another
    ctx.strokeStyle="blue";
    ctx.lineWidth=10;
    ctx.strokeRect(100,60,80,130);
  }
}
```

How it works...

This is what you can observe in the output of the recipe:

- The top-most blue bordered rectangle is drawn using the `strokeRect()` function
- The second red colored rectangle is drawn using the `fillRect()` function
- The first green colored rectangle is drawn using the `rect()` and `fill()` functions

The property `fillStyle` decides the color for filling the rectangle. The `strokeStyle` property decides the color of the border.

The three rectangles drawing functions accept the following parameters:

Parameter	Description
X	The x coordinate of the upper-left corner of the rectangle
Y	The y coordinate of the upper-left corner of the rectangle
Width	The width (in pixels) of the rectangle
Height	The height (in pixels) of the rectangle

Diagrammatically it can be shown as follows:

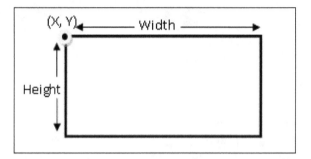

Drawing triangles

There is no direct function to draw a triangle using the canvas API. But we do have the other, simpler functions that, together, allow us to draw different shapes. A triangle is a combination of three joined lines. Let's see this in our new example. The output is quite simple and looks like this:

Triangles

How to do it...

The triangle is drawn by calling two basic functions, namely `moveTo()` and `lineTo()`. Here is the recipe.

The HTML file:

```html
<html>
<head>
<title>triangles</title>
<script src="triangles.js"></script>
</head>
<body onload="init()">
<canvas id="MyCanvasArea" width="200" height="200" style="border:2px
solid blue;" >
      your browser does not support canvas
</canvas>
<H1>Triangle</H1>
</body>
</html>
```

The JavaScript file:

```javascript
function init(){
  var can = document.getElementById("MyCanvasArea");
  if(can.getContext)
  {
    var context=can.getContext("2d");
    drawTriangle(context,100,20,100,100,"forestgreen");
  }
}
function drawTriangle(ctx, x, y,Width,Height,color){
  ctx.beginPath();
  ctx.moveTo(x, y);
  ctx.lineTo(x + Width / 2, y + Height);
  ctx.lineTo(x - Width / 2, y + Height);
  ctx.closePath();
  ctx.fillStyle = color;
  ctx.fill();
}
```

How it works...

The init() function calls the drawTriangle() method. The parameters passed for drawing the triangle are the X position, Y position, the width and height of the triangle, and the color for filling the triangle. The triangle drawing starts by calling the beginPath() function and ends on the call of the endPath() function. The moveTo() function takes you to the position from where you want to draw the triangle. Then, using the width and height, a line is drawn using the simple lineTo() function. Another line is drawn from there. The closePath() function completes the triangle by joining the last coordinate with the first one. The fillStyle property and fill() method does the job of filling the triangle with a color.

There's more...

Try the following:

- Instead of filling the triangle, only draw the triangle with boundaries. Use strokeStyle and stroke() before closePath().
- Place the stroke() method call after closePath() and check the output.

Drawing circles

Again, there is no direct function to draw a circle. It should be drawn using the function for drawing an arc. We saw a drawing of a circle in the previous chapter through the example of drawing arc2. The output of the circle recipe looks like this:

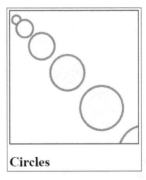

Circles

How to do it...

The recipe is very simple. It calls the `drawCircle()` function in a loop to draw multiple circles as you see here. The recipe is as follows.

The HTML code:

```html
<html>
<head>
<title>circles</title>
<script src="circles.js"></script>
</head>
<body onload="init()">
<canvas id="MyCanvasArea" width="300" height="300" style="border:2px
solid blue;" >
   your browser does not support canvas
</canvas>
<h1>Circles</h1>
</body>
</html>
```

The JavaScript code:

```javascript
function init(){
  var can=document.getElementById("MyCanvasArea");
  var ctx=can.getContext("2d");
  //call to the function to draw Circle
  for(i=1,x=15,y=20,r=10;i<=6;i++,x+=r*2,y+=r*2,r=r+10){
    drawCircle(ctx,x,y,r,"forestgreen","lightyellow");
  }
}
function drawCircle(ctx,xPos, yPos, radius, borderColor, fillColor){

    var startAngle =   0 * (Math.PI/180);
    var endAngle   = 360 * (Math.PI/180);

    var radius = radius;

    ctx.strokeStyle = borderColor;
    ctx.fillStyle   = fillColor;
    ctx.lineWidth   = 5;

    ctx.beginPath();
    ctx.arc(xPos, yPos, radius, startAngle, endAngle, false);
    ctx.fill();
    ctx.stroke();
  }
```

How it works...

The init() function calls the drawCircle() function, which in turn calls the arc() function with the necessary parameters to draw an arc from 0 degrees to 360 degrees, which completes a circle. Since the start and end angle to be passed in the arc() method must be in radians, the degrees are converted to radians. The formula used is: *radian = degree * π/180*. The border color and fill style are also specified.

The *x* and *y* coordinates and the radius value are specified in the for loop. The loop runs six times, drawing six circles at different positions and of different sizes. In every iteration, the value of x, y, and r changes (namely, the position and radius).

There's more...

Try the following:

- ▶ Remove the statement x+=r*2 and see the output
- ▶ Remove the statement y+=r*2 and see the output
- ▶ Remove the statement r=r+10 and see the output
- ▶ Change the border color and fill color

Drawing gradients

Here we implement some effects. Applying a gradient is quite a colorful activity. The output of our recipe demonstrating gradients looks like this:

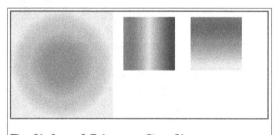

Radial and Linear Gradient

How to do it...

The recipe uses four new methods, namely `createRadialGradient()`, `createLinearGradient()`, `addColorStop()`, and `rgb()`. The recipe is as follows.

The HTML code:

```
<html>
<head>
<title>Gradients</title>
<script src="gradients.js"></script>
</head>
<body onload="init()">
<canvas id="MyCanvasArea" width="500" height="200" style="border:2px
solid blue;" >
your browser does not support canvas</canvas>
<h1>Radial and Linear Gradient</h1>
</body>
</html>
```

The JavaScript code:

```
function init()
{
  var can=document.getElementById("MyCanvasArea");
  var ctx=can.getContext("2d");

  //coordinates of center of 1st circle and a radius
  var x1 = 100;   // x of 1. circle center point
  var y1 = 100;   // y of 1. circle center point
  var r1 = 30;    // radius of 1. circle
  //coordinates of center of 2nd circle and a larger radius
  var x2 = 100;
  var y2 = 100;
  var r2 = 100;
  var radGrad=ctx.createRadialGradient(x1,y1,r1,x2,y2,r2);
  radGrad.addColorStop(0,'rgb(110,120, 255)');//bluish shade
  radGrad.addColorStop(0.5,'rgb(255,155,20)');//orange shade
  radGrad.addColorStop(1,'rgb(0, 255,220)');//green shade
  ctx.fillStyle = radGrad;
  ctx.fillRect(0,0, 200,200);

  //drawing the horizontal linear gradient
  var linGrad1 = ctx.createLinearGradient(220,0,320,0);
  linGrad1.addColorStop(0,'rgb(255,0,0)');//red
```

```
        linGrad1.addColorStop(0.5,'rgb(0,255,0)');//green
        linGrad1.addColorStop(1,'rgb(0,0,255)');//blue
        ctx.fillStyle = linGrad1;
        ctx.fillRect(220,10,100, 100);

        //drawing the vertical linear gradient
        var linGrad2 = ctx.createLinearGradient(0,0,0,100);
        linGrad2.addColorStop(0   , 'rgb(255,0,110)');
        linGrad2.addColorStop(0.5, 'rgb(0,110,255)');
        linGrad2.addColorStop(1   , 'rgb(110,255,0)');

        ctx.fillStyle = linGrad2;
        ctx.fillRect(350, 10, 100, 100);
    }
```

How it works...

The new methods and their purpose are listed in the following table:

Function	Description
`addColorStop(offset,color)`	This method can be called for a gradient to add the color and the value of offset (between 0 and 1) to indicate the percentage of color to be applied in the area specified for the gradient.
`createLinearGradient(xPos1,yPos1,xPos2,yPos2)`	This function allows the creation of the area in which the gradient can be applied. The area can be created by specifying the coordinates. Note: If `x1` and `x2` are the same then the vertical gradient can be applied. If `y1` and `y2` are the same, a horizontal gradient can be applied.
`createRadialGradient(x1,y1,r1,x2,y2,r2)`	(`x1,y1`) is the center of the starting circle and (`x2,y2`) is center of the ending circle. `r1` and `r2` are the radius of these two circles.
`rgb(value_for_red,value_for_green,value_for_blue)`	The value for any of the colors can be an integer between 0 and 255. The combination of these three colors creates the resultant color and can be applied in the `addColorStop()` function.

Radial gradient

Observe the first rectangle in the output, and you will understand that at the center of the circle there is a bluish shade. The next concentric circle has an orange shade, and towards the outer side of the circle you will observe a greenish shade. This is because of the following snippet:

```
radGrad.addColorStop(0,'rgb(110,120, 255)');//bluish shade
  radGrad.addColorStop(0.5,'rgb(255,155,20)');//orange shade
  radGrad.addColorStop(1,'rgb(0, 255,220)');//green shade
```

But then, what is **radGrad**? `radGrad` is the radial gradient created using the arguments specifying the centers of two circles (starting and ending) and their radius. `radGrad` is created by calling the `createRadialGradient()` function.

Linear gradient

The linear gradient is created by calling the `createLinearGradient()` function. The function allows specifying the starting coordinate and the ending coordinate. This defines a rectangular portion where the gradient is applied. Any drawing in this area will be filled with the gradient colors available in that area. If the drawing is drawn beyond the gradient area, then the color towards that end of the gradient will be applied to the drawing. You will definitely understand this paragraph when you see our next recipe.

In the current recipe there are two types of gradient, namely **horizontal** and **vertical**.

The following code applies the horizontal gradient:

```
var linGrad1 = ctx.createLinearGradient(220,0,320,0);
  linGrad1.addColorStop(0,'rgb(255,0,0)');//red
  linGrad1.addColorStop(0.5,'rgb(0,255,0)');//green
  linGrad1.addColorStop(1,'rgb(0,0,255)');//blue
```

Observe the coordinates. The `y1` and `y2` values are the same. It means that the gradient is along the *x* axis, the width being `100(320-220)`. So the `red`, `green`, and `blue` colors are applied in this region. Now, a rectangle with an *x* coordinate between `220` and `320` is drawn on the canvas, and can be filled with the gradient specified previously. This is done by the following code in our recipe:

```
ctx.fillStyle = linGrad1;
  ctx.fillRect(220,10,100, 100);
```

 Note that the coordinates of the rectangle starting from `220, 10` are inside the region specified in the gradient `linGrad1`.

Technically, the vertical gradient is not much different from the horizontal gradient. Here, the *x* values of both the coordinates specified in the `createLinearGradient()` function are the same, while the *y* values differ, specifying the region along the *y* axis.

Try the following:

- ▸ For the radial gradient, change the value of y2 (y value of the center coordinates of the second circle) to 50
- ▸ Change the values in the rgb() function

Working with custom shapes and styles

Until now we have learned how to draw basic shapes such as lines, arcs, curves, andrectangles. However, using this knowledge you can draw various shapes, such as a pentagon, a hexagon, a cloud, and so on. Our new recipe shows you how. In addition, it also shows you the different ways of filling these shapes with different effects:

The output of our recipe is as follows:

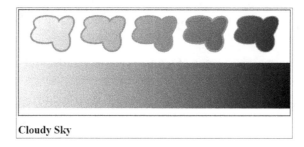

Cloudy Sky

How to do it...

The recipe is given as follows.

The HTML code:

```
<html>
<head>
<title>Clouds</title>
<script src="clouds.js"></script>
</head>
<body onload="init()">
<canvas id="MyCanvasArea" width="800" height="300" style="border:2px
solid blue;" >
your browser does not support canvas</canvas>
<h1>Cloudy Sky</h1>
</body>
</html>
```

The JavaScript code:

```
var can;
var ctx;
var color;
function init()
{
  can=document.getElementById("MyCanvasArea");
  ctx=can.getContext("2d");

  //set the gradient
  color=ctx.createLinearGradient(0, 0, can.width, can.height);
  color.addColorStop(0,'white');
  color.addColorStop(0.5,'grey');
  color.addColorStop(1,'black');

  //draw the first cloud
  var xfactor=0;
  drawCloud(xfactor);

  //draw the second cloud
  xfactor=150;
  drawCloud(xfactor);

  //draw third cloud
  xfactor=xfactor+150;
  drawCloud(xfactor);

  //draw the fourth cloud
  xfactor=xfactor+150;
  drawCloud(xfactor);

  //draw the fourth cloud
  xfactor=xfactor+150;
  drawCloud(xfactor);

  //rectangle to just show the gradient
  ctx.rect(0,150,can.width,130);
  ctx.fill();
}

function drawCloud(xfactor)
{
      ctx.beginPath();
```

```
ctx.moveTo(50+xfactor,50);
ctx.bezierCurveTo(0+xfactor,100,100+xfactor,100,100+xfactor,90);
ctx.bezierCurveTo(100+xfactor,130,170+xfactor,130,
150+xfactor,70);
ctx.bezierCurveTo(190+xfactor,10,140+xfactor,10,120+xfactor,30);
ctx.bezierCurveTo(120+xfactor,10,20+xfactor,10,50+xfactor,50);
ctx.closePath();
ctx.fillStyle=color;
ctx.fill();
ctx.lineWidth = 5;
ctx.strokeStyle = 'grey';
ctx.stroke();
}
```

How it works...

The function `drawCloud()` is called multiple times in the code. The `xfactor` variable is changed to shift the cloud along the *x* axis.

Demonstrating translation, rotation, and scaling

These three 2D transformation techniques are quite useful:

▸ **Translation** means changing the position of the origin `(0,0)` of the context

▸ **Rotation** means moving the context by a particular angle

▸ **Scaling** means changing the size of the drawing along the *x* axis and/or along the *y* axis

All three techniques are demonstrated in our new recipe whose output looks like this:

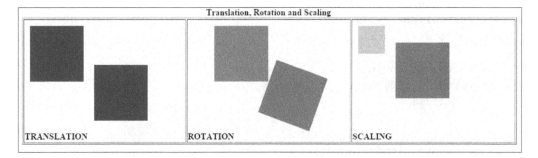

How to do it...

The following code does the job.

The HTML code:

```
<html>
<head>
<title>Translate, rotate and scale</title>
<script src="TRS.js"></script>
</head>
<body onload="drawTRS();">
<table border="1" align="center" bgcolor="lightyellow">
  <caption><b>Translation, Rotation and Scaling</b></caption>
<tr>
<td><canvas id="can0" width="300" height="200"></canvas><br/>
<b><label id="lbl0"></label></b>
</td>

<td><canvas id="can1" width="300" height="200"></canvas><br/>
<b><label id="lbl1"></label></b>
</td>

<td><canvas id="can2" width="300" height="200"></canvas><br/>
<b><label id="lbl2"></label></b>
</td>
</tr>
</table>
</body>
</html>
```

The JavaScript code:

```
function drawTRS(){
  var label0 = document.createTextNode('TRANSLATION');
   document.getElementById('lbl0').appendChild(label0);
   var ctx0 = document.getElementById('can0').getContext('2d');
  ctx0.fillStyle="blue";
  ctx0.fillRect(10,10,100,100);
  ctx0.translate(120,70);     //translation
  ctx0.fillRect(10,10,100,100);

  var label1 = document.createTextNode('ROTATION');
   document.getElementById('lbl1').appendChild(label1);
```

```
    var ctx1 = document.getElementById('can1').getContext('2d');
ctx1.fillStyle="red";
ctx1.fillRect(50,10,100,100);
ctx1.rotate(20*Math.PI/180);//rotate by 20 degrees
ctx1.fillStyle="green";
ctx1.fillRect(180,10,100,100);

    var label2 = document.createTextNode('SCALING');
    document.getElementById('lbl2').appendChild(label2);
    var ctx2 = document.getElementById('can2').getContext('2d');
ctx2.fillStyle="yellowgreen";
ctx2.fillRect(10,10,50,50);
ctx2.scale(2,2);     //scaling
ctx2.fillStyle="crimson";
ctx2.fillRect(40,20,50,50);
}
```

How it works...

There are three different functions to do these three tasks of translation, rotation, and scaling:

- ▶ The translation happens by calling the `translate(xPos,yPos)` function. This shifts the origin of the context, for example `(0,0)`, to other coordinates as specified in the function. In our case it is `(120,70)`. This coordinate is considered as the origin and then the shape is drawn. Note that the coordinates passed in both the `fillRect()` function with respect to the context `ctx0` are the same.

- ▶ The rotation happens by calling the `rotate(angle)` function. The angle has to be in radians. Calls to this function shift the origin in an angular direction, depending on the value. In our recipe, the angle is `20` degrees and the shift is clockwise.

    Just imagine pressing both of your palms on a sheet of paper and moving your hands in a clockwise direction by a small angle. Thus, the paper will also change its angle.

- ▶ Scaling happens by calling one simple function named `scale(xScale,yScale)`. The parameters passed in this function decide the change in size along the x axis and the y axis. The values can be fractional. In our recipe the scaling is twice the original size.

There's more...

Try the following:

- ▶ Change the parameters of `translate`, `rotate`, and `scale` functions in the given recipe.

Drawing an ellipse

Drawing an ellipse is just an implementation of translation and scaling. The output is quite simple:

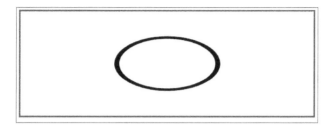

How to do it...

The recipe goes like this.

The HTML code:

```
<!DOCTYPE HTML>
<html>
<head>
</head>
<body onload="init()">
<canvas id="myCanvas" width="578" height="200" style="border:3px solid
blue"></canvas>
<script src="ellipse.js">
</script>
</body>
</html>
```

The JavaScript code:

```
function init()
{
      var canvas = document.getElementById('myCanvas');
      var context = canvas.getContext('2d');
      var centerX = 0;
      var centerY = 0;
      var radius = 50;
      // translate context
      context.translate(canvas.width / 2, canvas.height / 2);
      // scale context horizontally
      context.scale(2, 1);
```

```
        // draw circle which will be stretched into an ellipse
        context.beginPath();
        context.arc(centerX, centerY, radius, 0, 2 * Math.PI, false);

        context.lineWidth = 5;
        context.strokeStyle = 'black';
        context.stroke();
}
```

How it works...

Observe that the translate() and scale() functions are used to do this drawing. First, the origin is shifted by using the translate() function. Later, the scaling is applied. And then a circle is drawn using the arc() function.

Saving and restoring canvas state

This recipe is based on the concept of stack. You can imagine a stack of books. Say, for example, I have to pick up a book from a stack of three books. It's always logical and easy to pick up the top-most book, read it, and keep it aside. Then I pick another book from the two-book stack, read it, and keep it aside. Then I pick the last book, read it, and keep it aside.

States of canvas work in a similar way. Let's see the output of the recipe:

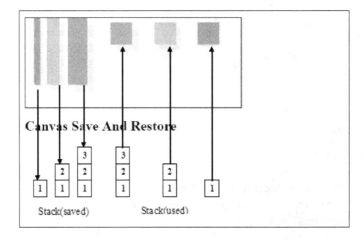

How to do it...

The recipe for the previous output goes like this.

The HTML code:

```html
<html>
<head>
<title>Canvas Save And Restore</title>
<script src="CanvasSaveRestore.js"></script>
</head>
<body onload="CanvasSaveRestore()">
<canvas id="MyCanvasArea" width="500" height="200" style="border:2px
solid blue;" >
   your browser does not support canvas
</canvas>
<h1>Canvas Save And Restore</h1>
</body>
</html>
```

The JavaScript code:

```javascript
function CanvasSaveRestore()
{
  can=document.getElementById("MyCanvasArea");
  ctx=can.getContext("2d");

  ctx.fillStyle = 'cadetblue';
  ctx.shadowOffsetX = 5;
  ctx.shadowOffsetY = 5;
  ctx.shadowBlur    = 4;
  ctx.shadowColor   = 'rgba(204, 204, 204, 0.5)';
  ctx.fillRect(20,0,15,150);
  ctx.save();

  ctx.fillStyle = 'burlywood';
  ctx.shadowOffsetX = 10;
  ctx.shadowOffsetY = 10;
  ctx.shadowBlur    = 4;
  ctx.shadowColor   = 'rgba(204, 204, 204, 0.5)';
  ctx.fillRect(50,0,30,150);
  ctx.save();
```

```
ctx.fillStyle = 'coral';
ctx.shadowOffsetX = 15;
ctx.shadowOffsetY = 15;
ctx.shadowBlur    = 4;
ctx.shadowColor   = 'rgba(204, 204, 204, 0.5)';
ctx.fillRect(100,0,45,150);
ctx.save();

ctx.restore();
ctx.beginPath();
ctx.rect(200,10,50,50);
ctx.closePath();
ctx.fill();

ctx.restore();
ctx.beginPath();
ctx.rect(300,10,50,50);
ctx.closePath();
ctx.fill();

ctx.restore();
ctx.beginPath();
ctx.rect(400,10,50,50);
ctx.closePath();
ctx.fill();

}
```

How it works...

The first rectangle is drawn using certain styles and effects. This state of canvas is stored in the stack at position 1 (refer to the output). Then the other rectangle is drawn with different settings and this state is saved at position 2, which is above 1. The same happens with the third triangle. The saving of state happens using the `save()` method.

While restoring the state of canvas from the stack, whatever is on the top of the stack is removed and used. So the state at position 3 on the stack is used to draw the next rectangle. The next rectangle then uses the state at position 2, as the state at position 3 has already been removed and used. Finally, the state stored at position 1 is used to draw the last rectangle.

Demonstrating composites

Composite operations allow you to change how the new content is drawn on an HTML5 <canvas> element. New things appear over whatever has already been drawn. By changing the global composite operation, you can draw new shapes behind existing ones, perform boolean operations, and do some other neat things.

The two main components in a compositing operation are the **destination** and the **source**. The destination is what is already on the canvas, and the source is what is getting drawn onto the canvas.

The following is a description for each possible composite operation available with the HTML5 Canvas API, where the text *Be happy* represents the source (**S**), and the *green rectangle* represents the destination (**D**). To further develop your understanding of composite operations, it helps to look at the corresponding operation while reading each description:

Operation	Description
source-atop (S atop D)	Display the source image wherever both images are opaque. Display the destination image wherever the destination image is opaque but the source image is transparent. Display transparency elsewhere.
source-in (S in D)	Display the source image wherever both the source image and destination image are opaque. Display transparency elsewhere.
source-out (S out D)	Display the source image wherever the source image is opaque and the destination image is transparent. Display transparency elsewhere.
source-over (S over D, default)	Display the source image wherever the source image is opaque. Display the destination image elsewhere.
destination-atop (S atop D)	Display the destination image wherever both images are opaque. Display the source image wherever the source image is opaque but the destination image is transparent. Display transparency elsewhere.
destination-in (S in D)	Display the destination image wherever both the destination image and source image are opaque. Display transparency elsewhere.
destination-out (S out D)	Display the destination image wherever the destination image is opaque and the source image is transparent. Display transparency elsewhere.
destination-over (S over D)	Display the destination image wherever the destination image is opaque. Display the destination image elsewhere.

Operation	Description
`lighter` (S plus D)	Display the sum of the source image and destination image.
`xor` (S xor D)	Exclusive OR of the source image and destination image.
`copy` (D is ignored)	Display the source image instead of the destination image.

In short, the composites operate like this:

`source-over`	destination + source
`destination-over`	source + destination
`source-in`	destination & source
`destination-in`	source & destination
`source-out`	source – destination
`destination-out`	destination – source
`source-atop`	destination + (source & destination)
`destination-atop`	source + (destination & source)
`lighter`	destination + source + lighter (source & destination)
`darker`	destination + source + darker (source & destination)
`xor`	source ^ destination
`copy`	source

Let's see the output to understand the different composite types:

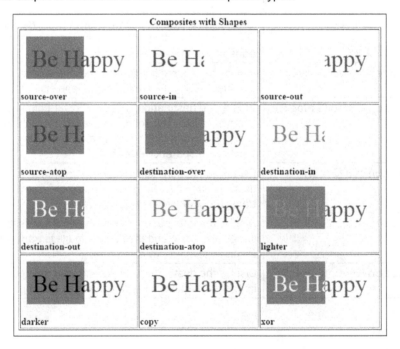

How to do it...

The recipe goes like this.

The HTML code:

```
<html>
<head>
<title>Composites</title>
<script src="composites.js"></script>
</head>
<body onload="drawComposites();">
<table border="1" align="center" bgcolor="lightyellow">
  <caption><b>Composites with Shapes</b></caption>
<tr>
<td><canvas id="can0" width="200" height="100"></canvas><br/>
<b><label id="lbl0"></label></b>
</td>

<td><canvas id="can1" width="200" height="100"></canvas><br/>
<b><label id="lbl1"></label></b>
</td>

<td><canvas id="can2" width="200" height="100"></canvas><br/>
<b><label id="lbl2"></label></b>
</td>
</tr>

<tr>
<td><canvas id="can3" width="200" height="100"></canvas><br/>
<b><label id="lbl3"></label></b>
</td>

<td><canvas id="can4" width="200" height="100"></canvas><br/>
<b><label id="lbl4"></label></b>
</td>

<td><canvas id="can5" width="200" height="100"></canvas><br/>
<b><label id="lbl5"></label></b>
</td>
</tr>
```

```
<tr>
<td><canvas id="can6" width="200" height="100"></canvas><br/>
<b><label id="lbl6"></label><b>
</td>

<td><canvas id="can7" width="200" height="100"></canvas><br/>
<b><label id="lbl7"></label></b>
</td>

<td><canvas id="can8" width="200" height="100"></canvas><br/>
<b><label id="lbl8"></label></b>
</td>
</tr>

<tr>
<td><canvas id="can9" width="200" height="100"></canvas><br/>
<b><label id="lbl9"></label></b>
</td>

<td><canvas id="can10" width="200" height="100"></canvas><br/>
<b><label id="lbl10"></label></b>
</td>

<td><canvas id="can11" width="200" height="100"></canvas><br/>
<b><label id="lbl11"></label></b>
</td>
</tr>
</table>
</body>
</html>
```

The JavaScript code:

```
var compositeTypes = ['source-over','source-in','source-
out','source-atop','destination-over','destination-in','destination-
out','destination-atop','lighter','darker','copy','xor'];
function drawComposites(){
    for (i=0;i<compositeTypes.length;i++){
      var label = document.createTextNode(compositeTypes[i]);
document.getElementById('lbl'+i).appendChild(label);
      var ctx = document.getElementById('can'+i).getContext('2d');
      ctx.fillStyle="green";
      ctx.fillRect(10,10,100,70);
      ctx.globalCompositeOperation = compositeTypes[i];
```

```
        ctx.fillStyle="blue";
        ctx.font="40px ComicSans";
        ctx.fillText("Be Happy",20,60);
    }
}
```

How it works...

The HTML code contains a table of four rows and three columns, thereby producing 12 cells (0 to 11). There is a canvas and label element in each of the cells (within the `<TD>` tag). These elements are captured in the JavaScript code in a loop that iterates for every composition type. The types are mentioned in the array, and the `globalCompositeOperation` property is assigned with the composite type before drawing the source.

Drawing a mouse

This recipe is an implementation of multiple functions demonstrated so far. The output looks like this:

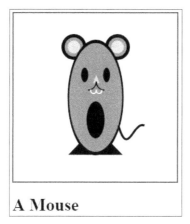

A Mouse

How to do it...

The recipe is as follows.

The HTML code:

```
<html>
<head>
<title>Mouse</title>
<script src="mouse.js"></script>
</head>
```

```
<body onload="init()">
<canvas id="MyCanvasArea" width="300" height="300" style="border:2px
solid blue;" >
   your browser does not support canvas
</canvas>
<h1>A Mouse</h1>
</body>
</html>
```

The JavaScript code:

```
function init()
{
  var can=document.getElementById("MyCanvasArea");
  var ctx=can.getContext("2d");
  drawCircle(ctx,110,60,20,6,"black","grey");
  drawCircle(ctx,110,60,10,3,"pink","pink");
  drawCircle(ctx,190,60,20,6,"black","grey");
  drawCircle(ctx,190,60,10,3,"pink","pink");
  drawTriangle(ctx,150,202.4,100,50,"black");
  ctx.save();
  ctx.translate(can.width/2,can.height/2);
  ctx.scale(1,2);
  ctx.save();

  ctx.restore();
  drawCircle(ctx,0,0,50,3,"black","grey");
  drawCircle(ctx,-20,-20,5,3,"black","black");
  drawCircle(ctx,20,-20,5,3,"black","black");
  drawCircle(ctx,0,20,15,3,"black","black");
  ctx.restore();
  drawTriangle(ctx,151,110,12,15,"pink");
  drawArc(ctx,166,122,15,90,180,false,"black","grey");
  drawArc(ctx,136,122,15,0,90,false,"black","grey");
  drawArc(ctx,146,138,5,-15,200,false,"white","grey");
  drawArc(ctx,156,138,5,-15,200,false,"white","grey");
  drawBezierCurve(ctx,192,200,210,260,220,190,240,200,"black");
}

function drawCircle(ctx,xPos, yPos, radius,borderwidth, borderColor,
fillColor){
      var startAngle =    0 * (Math.PI/180);
      var endAngle   = 360 * (Math.PI/180);
      var radius = radius;
```

```
        ctx.strokeStyle = borderColor;
        ctx.fillStyle   = fillColor;
        ctx.lineWidth   = borderwidth;

        ctx.beginPath();
        ctx.arc(xPos, yPos, radius, startAngle, endAngle, false);
        ctx.fill();
        ctx.stroke();
}
function drawArc(ctx,xPos,yPos,radius,startAngle,endAngle,
anticlockwise,lineColor, fillColor){
   var startAngle = startAngle * (Math.PI/180);
   var endAngle   = endAngle   * (Math.PI/180);
   var radius = radius;

   ctx.strokeStyle = lineColor;
   ctx.fillStyle   = fillColor;
   ctx.lineWidth   = 2;
   ctx.beginPath();
   ctx.arc(xPos,yPos,radius,startAngle,endAngle,anticlockwise);
   ctx.fill();
   ctx.stroke();
}
function drawTriangle(ctx, x, y,Width,Height,color){
   ctx.beginPath();
   ctx.moveTo(x, y);
   ctx.lineTo(x + Width / 2, y + Height);
   ctx.lineTo(x - Width / 2, y + Height);
   ctx.closePath();
   ctx.fillStyle = color;
   ctx.fill();
}
function drawBezierCurve(ctx,xstart,ystart,xctrl1,yctrl1,xctrl2,yctrl2
,xend,yend,color){
   ctx.strokeStyle=color;
   ctx.lineWidth=4;
   ctx.beginPath();
   ctx.moveTo(xstart,ystart);
   ctx.bezierCurveTo(xctrl1,yctrl1,xctrl2,yctrl2,xend,yend);
   ctx.stroke();
}
```

How it works...

The previous recipe follows these steps:

1. The different shapes to be sent behind the larger ellipse are drawn first.
2. Then the translation and scaling is applied so that ellipses can be drawn.
3. The state is restored and then the remaining shapes are drawn above the larger ellipse.

Observe that the coordinates used before translation and scaling differ from those used after the effects.

3
Animation

This chapter explains the process of animation and demonstrates the same. In this chapter we will cover:

- ▶ Creating an animation class
- ▶ Demonstrating acceleration
- ▶ Demonstrating gravity
- ▶ Animating a line
- ▶ Animating text
- ▶ Animating a clock
- ▶ Animating a solar system
- ▶ Animating particles
- ▶ Animating a particle fountain
- ▶ Animating a rain effect
- ▶ Animating a snow effect

Introduction

This chapter explains the basic animation process. This is one of the most important aspects of HTML5 and is achieved through JavaScript. The chapter is loaded with recipes for various animations.

Creating an animation class

As per Wikipedia, **animation** is the process of creating the illusion of motion and shape change by means of the rapid display of a sequence of static images that minimally differ from each other. So we draw a canvas, clear it, then draw it again with minimal changes, again clear it, again draw it with some more changes, again clear it, and this cycle continues.

So the steps for animation can be given as:

1. Initialize.
2. Clear the canvas.
3. Draw on the canvas.
4. Update the drawing with minimum changes.
5. Perform the previous three steps (2, 3 4) in a loop.

These steps need to be called rapidly, and for this we use a function named `requireanimationframe` (callback).

This method tells the browser that you wish to perform an animation and requests that the browser calls a specified function to update an animation before the next repaint (redraw). The method takes as an argument a callback method to be invoked before the repaint (redraw).

As browsers and computer hardware are not created equally, it's important to understand that the optimal **FPS (frames per second)** value for each animation varies depending on the browser, the computer's hardware, and the animation's algorithm.

Demonstrating acceleration

Here is a simple recipe demonstrating the physics principle of acceleration. The output looks like this:

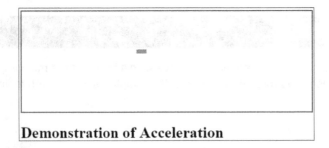

Demonstration of Acceleration

How to do it...

The recipe is as follows:

The HTML code:

```html
<html>
<head>
<title>Demonstration of Acceleration</title>
<script src="Acceleration.js"></script>
</head>
<body onload="init();">
<canvas id="MyCanvasArea" width="600" height="200" style="border:2px
solid blue;" >
   your browser does not support canvas
</canvas>
<h1>Demonstration of Acceleration</h1>
</body>
</html>
```

The JavaScript code:

```javascript
var x =  0;
var y;
var xEnd=600;
var goRight=true;
var can;
var ctx;
var acceleration=0.006;
var time=1;
function animate() {

    reqAnimFrame = window.mozRequestAnimationFrame    ||
            window.webkitRequestAnimationFrame ||
            window.msRequestAnimationFrame    ||
            window.oRequestAnimationFrame
            ;
    clear();    //clear the canvas
    updateLine(); //update the drawing
    drawLine();    //draw the drawing

    reqAnimFrame(animate);//loop the above mentioned steps
}
function updateLine()
{
    if(x<xEnd && goRight)
    {
```

```
        x=acceleration*time*time;
        time+=2;
        }
        if(x>=xEnd)
        {
          goRight=false;
        x=xEnd;
        }
    }
    function drawLine()
    {
        ctx.beginPath();
        ctx.strokeStyle = "rgba(255,0,0,0.8)";
        ctx.lineWidth=8;
        ctx.moveTo(x-20,y);
        ctx.lineTo(x,y);
        ctx.stroke();
    }
    function init() {
        can  = document.getElementById("MyCanvasArea");
        ctx = can.getContext("2d");
        y=can.height/2;
        animate();
    }

    function clear()
    {
      ctx.clearRect(0, 0, can.width, can.height);
    }
```

How it works...

The workings of this recipe are very simple. You have to repeat three simple steps,
which are; clear the canvas, update your drawing, and then draw it. The updateLine()
method changes the x position of the starting coordinate of the line. So before the line
is drawn, the line's starting position moves towards the right. This process happens in
a loop, which is taken care of by the reqAnimFrame() method, which calls back the
animate() method, which in turn calls the clear(), updateLine(), and drawLine()
methods. The RequestAnimationFrame is supported by different browsers under
different names; for example mozRequestAnimationFrame is for Mozilla Firefox,
WebKitRequestAnimationFrame is for Chrome and Safari, msRequestAnimationFrame
is for Internet Explorer, and oRequestAnimationFrame is for Opera. reqAnimFrame
picks the right one according to the browser you use.

The `init` method sets the value for the x coordinate and then calls the `animate` method. The value for acceleration is set and the time increments by 2 in every update. The starting coordinates of the line change as per the formula, in every update, and then the line is redrawn.

Demonstrating gravity

Gravity can be understood as acceleration along the *y* axis, otherwise known as things falling straight to the ground. The output of this recipe is shown as follows:

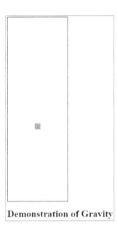

Demonstration of Gravity

How to do it...

This recipe is similar to the previous one. The recipe is as follows.

The HTML code:

```
<html>
<head>
<title>Demonstration of Gravity</title>
<script src="Gravity.js"></script>
</head>
<body onload="init();">
<canvas id="MyCanvasArea" width="200" height="600" style="border:2px
solid blue;" >
    your browser does not support canvas
</canvas>
<h1>Demonstration of Gravity</h1>
</body>
</html>
```

The JavaScript code:

```javascript
var x =  0;
var y = 80;
var yEnd=600;
var goDown=true;
//same as prior recipe
....
....
function animate() {
//same as prior recipe
....
....
}
function updateLine()
{
    if(y<yEnd && goDown)
    {
      y=acceleration*time*time;
      time+=2;
    }
    if(y>=yEnd)
    {
      goDown=false;
      y=yEnd;
    }
}
function drawLine()
{
    ....
ctx.lineWidth=20;
    ctx.moveTo(x,y-20);
    ....
}
function init() {
    ....
x=can.width/2;
    ....
}
....
....
```

How it works...

The working of this recipe is very similar to the previous example. Instead of controlling the movement towards the left, downward movement is controlled. This is done by changing the value of the y coordinate on every update.

Animating a line

This animated line recipe shows a very basic animation, in which the line moves to and fro. The output of the recipe is shown here:

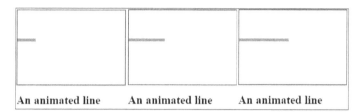

An animated line   An animated line   An animated line

How to do it...

The actual output is a single canvas with the animated line. The previous image tries to help you visualize the frames in different stages of the animation. You need to try this example to get a feel. The code is given as follows:

The HTML code:

```
<html>
<head>
<title>A simple line animation</title>
<script src="LineAnimation.js"></script>
</head>
<body onload="init();">
<canvas id="MyCanvasArea" width="300" height="200" style="border:2px
solid blue;" >
    your browser does not support canvas
</canvas>
<h1>An animated line</h1>
</body>
</html>
```

The JavaScript file, as mentioned in the `<script>` tag in the previous code:

```javascript
var x =   0;
var y = 80;
var xEnd=200;
var goRight=true;
var canvas;
var context;
function animate() {
reqAnimFrame = window.mozRequestAnimationFrame     ||
                window.webkitRequestAnimationFrame ||
                window.msRequestAnimationFrame     ||
                window.oRequestAnimationFrame;

clear();     //clear the canvas
drawLine();    //draw the drawing
updateLine();   //update the drawing

reqAnimFrame(animate);//loop the above mentioned steps
}
function updateLine(){
    if(x<xEnd && goRight)
    {
    x+=2;
    }
    else if(x>0 && !goRight)
    {
    x-=2;
    }
    if(x==xEnd)
    goRight=false;
    else if(x==0)
    goRight=true;
}
function drawLine(){
    context.beginPath();
    context.strokeStyle = "rgba(255,0,0,0.8)";
    context.lineWidth=8;
    context.moveTo(0,y);
    context.lineTo(x,y);
    context.stroke();
}
function init() {
    canvas  = document.getElementById("MyCanvasArea");
```

```
    context = canvas.getContext("2d");
    animate();
}
function clear()
{
  context.clearRect(0, 0, canvas.width, canvas.height);
  }
```

How it works...

The HTML file calls the `init()` function, as mentioned for the `onload` event. Observe the method calls made in the `animate()` function. They are `init()`, `clear()`, `draw()`, and `update()`. With a rate of `60` FPS, the `reqAnimFrame()` function calls back the three functions, namely `clear()`, `drawLine()`, and `updateLine()` in a loop.

The purpose of each function is given as follows:

Name of the function	Purpose
`init()`	Initializes the canvas.
`clear()`	Clears the area you desire. In this recipe it clears the whole canvas.
`drawLine()`	Method to draw a line.
`updateLine()`	Updates the coordinates to show a bigger line each time up to certain coordinates, after which it gets shorter and shorter till it reaches the starting point.
`animate()`	This function executes the animation cycle.
`reqAnimFrame()`	This is a function created as per your browser and it calls the `animate()` function with a rate of `60` FPS. In turn `animate()` calls functions 2, 3, 4, and 5 in a loop.

There's more...

Try the following:

- Replace `200` at both places in the program with `300`
- Call the `updateLine()` method before the `drawLine()` method
- Change `moveTo(0,y)` to `moveTo(x-20,y)`

Animating text

It gives immense pleasure when you see your name on a screen. And it looks much better when animated. After learning this recipe, try your name.

You have seen the animation of a shape. The new recipe shows the animation of some text. The output is shown here:

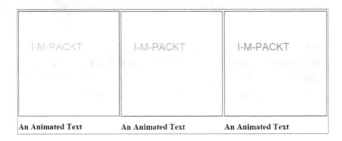

How to do it...

This recipe is very similar to the code shown in the first recipe.

The HTML code:

```
<html>
<head>
<title>Animated Text</title>
<script src="TextAnim.js"></script>
</head>
<body onload="init();">
<canvas id="MyCanvasArea" width="400" height="400" style="border:2px
solid blue;" >
    your browser does not support canvas
</canvas>
<h1>An Animated Text</h1>
</body>
</html>
```

The JavaScript code:

```
var can;
var ctx;
var alpha=0.0;
var goUp=true;
```

```
function animate() {
  reqAnimFrame = window.mozRequestAnimationFrame     ||
                 window.webkitRequestAnimationFrame ||
                 window.msRequestAnimationFrame     ||
                 window.oRequestAnimationFrame;
  clear();
  drawText();
  updateText();
  reqAnimFrame(animate);
}
function init(){....}  //refer previous recipe
function clear(){....}//refer previous recipe
function drawText() {
  ctx.font = "30pt Arial";
  ctx.fillStyle="rgba(255,0,0,"+alpha+")";
  ctx.fillText('I-M-PACKT',50,150);
}
function updateText(){
  if(alpha>=1.0)
    goUp=false;
  else if(alpha<=0.1)
    goUp=true;

  if(alpha>=0.0 && goUp)
  {
    alpha=alpha+0.01;
  }
  else if(alpha<=1.5 && !goUp)
  {
    alpha=alpha-0.01;
  }
}
```

How it works...

This recipe works on the same principle of an animation cycle. The only difference here is that text is drawn and the transparency parameter alpha is increased and reduced as an update before every subsequent drawing.

Try the following:

▶ Apply a shadow effect to the text

Animating a clock

An animated clock can be visualized easily. The output of this recipe is:

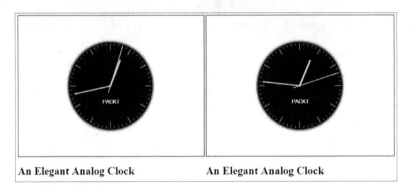

An Elegant Analog Clock   An Elegant Analog Clock

How to do it...

The recipe for the clock is as follows:

The HTML code:

```
<html>
<head>
<title>Animated Clock</title>
<script src="AnalogClock.js"></script>
</head>
<body onload="animate();">
<canvas id="MyCanvasArea" width="550" height="400" style="border:2px
solid blue;" >
    your browser does not support canvas
</canvas>
<h1>An Elegant Analog Clock</h1>
</body>
</html>
```

The JavaScript code:

```
function animate()
{
  reqAnimFrame = window.mozRequestAnimationFrame    ||
            window.webkitRequestAnimationFrame ||
            window.msRequestAnimationFrame    ||
            window.oRequestAnimationFrame
            ;

  showClock();
  reqAnimFrame(animate);
}
    function showClock() {

        // DEFINE CANVAS AND ITS CONTEXT.
        var can = document.getElementById('MyCanvasArea');
        var ctx = can.getContext('2d');

        var date = new Date;
        var angle;
        var secHandLength = 120;

      var cp=1;

// CLEAR EVERYTHING ON THE CANVAS. RE-DRAW NEW ELEMENTS EVERY SECOND.
//ctx.clearRect(0, 0, canvas.width, canvas.height);

        drawInnerDial();

    drawOuterDial();

    drawCenterDial();

        showHours();
        showSeconds();

        showSecondsHand();
        showMinutesHand();
        showHoursHand();
    nameTheClock();
  function drawOuterDial() {
            ctx.beginPath();
    ctx.lineWidth=4;
```

```
                    ctx.arc(can.width / 2, can.height / 2, secHandLength
                    + 10, 0, Math.PI * 2);
                    ctx.strokeStyle = '#00FFFF';
                    ctx.stroke();
            }
    function drawInnerDial() {
                    ctx.beginPath();
        ctx.lineWidth=5;
                    ctx.arc(can.width / 2, can.height / 2, secHandLength
                    + 7, 0, Math.PI * 2);
        ctx.fillStyle="rgba(0,0,0,0.2)";
        ctx.fill();
                    ctx.strokeStyle = "rgba(200,0,100,1)";
                    ctx.stroke();
            }
    function drawCenterDial() {
                    ctx.beginPath();
                    ctx.arc(can.width / 2, can.height / 2, 2, 0, Math.PI
                    * 2);
                    ctx.lineWidth = 3;
                    ctx.fillStyle = '#000000';
                    ctx.strokeStyle = 'rgba(200,100,50,0.5)';
                    ctx.stroke();
            }
        function showHours() {
                    for (var i = 0; i < 12; i++) {
                        angle = (i - 3) * (Math.PI * 2) / 12;
                        // THE ANGLE TO MARK.
                        ctx.lineWidth = 2;              // HAND WIDTH.
                        ctx.beginPath();

                        var x1 = (can.width / 2) + Math.cos(angle)
                        * (secHandLength);
                        var y1 = (can.height / 2) + Math.sin(angle)
                        * (secHandLength);
                        var x2 = (can.width / 2) + Math.cos(angle)
                        * (secHandLength - (secHandLength / 7));
                        var y2 = (can.height / 2) + Math.sin(angle)
                        * (secHandLength - (secHandLength / 7));

                        ctx.moveTo(x1, y1);
                        ctx.lineTo(x2, y2);

                        ctx.strokeStyle = '#FF0000';
                        ctx.stroke();
```

```
            }
        }
    }

function showSeconds() {

        for (var i = 0; i < 60; i++) {
            angle = (i - 3) * (Math.PI * 2) / 60;
            // THE ANGLE TO MARK.
            ctx.lineWidth = 1;              // HAND WIDTH.
            ctx.beginPath();

            var x1 = (can.width / 2) + Math.cos(angle)
            * (secHandLength);
            var y1 = (can.height / 2) + Math.sin(angle)
            * (secHandLength);
            var x2 = (can.width / 2) + Math.cos(angle)
            * (secHandLength - (secHandLength / 30));
            var y2 = (can.height / 2) + Math.sin(angle)
            * (secHandLength - (secHandLength / 30));

            ctx.moveTo(x1, y1);
            ctx.lineTo(x2, y2);

            ctx.strokeStyle = '#C4D1D5';
            ctx.stroke();
        }
    }

function showSecondsHand() {

        var sec = date.getSeconds();
        angle = ((Math.PI * 2) * (sec / 60)) - ((Math.PI * 2)
        / 4);
        ctx.lineWidth = 2;                 // HAND WIDTH.

        ctx.beginPath();
        ctx.moveTo(can.width / 2, can.height / 2);
        // START FROM CENTER OF THE CLOCK.
        ctx.lineTo((can.width / 2 + Math.cos(angle) *
        secHandLength),(can.height / 2 + Math.sin(angle) *
        secHandLength));

        // DRAW THE TAIL OF THE SECONDS HAND.
        ctx.moveTo(can.width / 2, can.height / 2);
```

```
                    ctx.lineTo((can.width / 2 - Math.cos(angle) *
                    20),(can.height / 2 - Math.sin(angle) * 20));

                    ctx.strokeStyle = '#FFAC00';
                    ctx.stroke();
            }
        function showMinutesHand() {

                    var min = date.getMinutes();
                    angle = ((Math.PI * 2) * (min / 60)) - ((Math.PI * 2)
                    / 4);
                    ctx.lineWidth = 3;

                    ctx.beginPath();
                    ctx.moveTo(can.width / 2, can.height / 2);
                    ctx.lineTo((can.width / 2 + Math.cos(angle) *
                    secHandLength / 1.1),(can.height / 2 + Math.sin(angle)
                    * secHandLength / 1.1));

                    ctx.strokeStyle = '#00FFAA';
                    ctx.stroke();
                }

            function showHoursHand() {

                    var hour = date.getHours();
                    var min = date.getMinutes();
                    angle = ((Math.PI * 2) * ((hour * 5 + (min / 60) * 5)
                    / 60)) - ((Math.PI * 2) / 4);
                    ctx.lineWidth = 4.5;

                    ctx.beginPath();
                    ctx.moveTo(can.width / 2, can.height / 2);
                    ctx.lineTo((can.width / 2 + Math.cos(angle) *
                    secHandLength / 1.5),(can.height / 2 + Math.sin(angle)
                    * secHandLength / 1.5));

                    ctx.strokeStyle = '#00FFAA';
                    ctx.stroke();
                }
        function nameTheClock()
        {
          ctx.font = "11pt Arial";
          ctx.fillStyle="white";
          ctx.fillText('PACKT',can.width/2-23,can.height/2+50);
        }
            }
```

How it works...

There are different functions that have been defined in JavaScript and then invoked repeatedly to do their respective tasks. The names of the functions explain their tasks.

The functions are `drawInnerDial()`, `drawOuterDial()`, `drawCenterDial()`, `showHours()`, `showSeconds()`, `showSecondsHand()`, `showMinutesHand()`, `showHoursHand()`, and `nameTheClock()`. The `cos()` and `sin()` functions do the trick of moving the hands with an appropriate angle.

Animating a solar system

The solar system has always been attractive to view for all ages. Here is a recipe for a solar system whose output can be shown as:

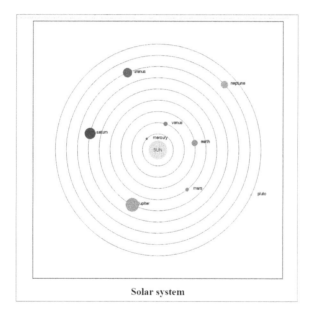

Solar system

How to do it...

The following is the recipe for the solar system:

The HTML code:

```
<html>
<head>
<title>Animated Solar System</title>
<script src="SolarSystem.js"></script>
```

```
</head>
<body onload="init();">
<center>
<canvas id="MyCanvasArea" width="800" height="800" style="border:2px
solid blue;" >
    your browser does not support canvas
</canvas>
<h1>Solar system</h1>
</center>
</body>
</html>
```

The JavaScript code:

```
var can;
var ctx;
var oradius,ocolor,pradius,pcolo,opradius,pcount;
var angshift=[0.009,0.008,0.007,0.006,0.005,0.009,0.005,0.006,0.007];
var ang=[60,80,100,120,140,160,180,200,220];
var colors=["blue","brown","green","crimson","olive","indigo","purple"
,"grey","red"];
var pradius=[3.5,7,10,6,22,18,15,12,2.8];
var pnames=["mercury","venus","earth","mars","jupiter","saturn","uranu
s","neptune","pluto"];
function animate()
{
   reqAnimFrame = window.mozRequestAnimationFrame    ||
                  window.webkitRequestAnimationFrame ||
                  window.msRequestAnimationFrame     ||
                  window.oRequestAnimationFrame
                  ;

   clear();
   setParams();
   drawSun();
   drawOrbits();
   drawPlanets();

   reqAnimFrame(animate);
}
function setParams()
{
   for(pcount=0;pcount<=9;pcount++)
   {
```

```
      ang[pcount]=ang[pcount]+angshift[pcount];
    }
}
function init()
{
  can=document.getElementById('MyCanvasArea');
  ctx=can.getContext("2d");

  // scale context horizontally
  ctx.scale(1, 1);
  animate();
}
function drawSun()
{
  ctx.beginPath();
  ctx.fillStyle='orange';
  ctx.arc(can.width/2, can.height/2, 30, 0, Math.PI*2, true);
  ctx.closePath();
  ctx.fill();
  ctx.beginPath();
  ctx.font = "10pt Arial";
  ctx.fillStyle="rgb(0,0,0)";
  ctx.fillText('SUN',can.width/2-15,can.height/2+5);
  ctx.closePath();
}
function drawOrbits()
{
  var i;
  oradius=15;
  for(i=1;i<=9;i++)
  {
    oradius=oradius+35;
    ocolor='black';
    ctx.beginPath();
    ctx.strokeStyle=ocolor;
    ctx.arc(can.width/2, can.height/2, oradius, 0, Math.PI*2, true);
    ctx.closePath();
    ctx.stroke();
  }
}
function drawPlanets()
{
  var x;
  var y;
```

```
    opradius=15;
    for(var i=0;i<=8;i++)
    {
        opradius=opradius+35;
        ctx.beginPath();
        ctx.fillStyle=colors[i];
        x=can.width/2+ opradius*Math.cos(ang[i]);
        y=can.height/2+Math.sin(ang[i])* opradius;
        ctx.arc(x,y, pradius[i], 0, Math.PI*2, true);
        ctx.strokeText(pnames[i],x+20,y);
        ctx.closePath();
        ctx.fill();
    }
}
function clear()
{
    ctx.clearRect(0,0,can.width,can.height);
}
```

How it works...

The method is quite simple. First, we draw the sun. Then we draw the orbits and then a planet on each orbit. Different methods named `drawSun()`, `drawOrbits()`, and `drawPlanets()` are called to do this.

Animating particles

This is one of the most important topics in animation, as all kinds of actions are taken care of using these tiny things called particles. Particles can move randomly, accelerate, fall due to gravity, collide, and so on. A few of these effects are covered in this chapter.

This recipe is a very basic recipe to clarify how to create and animate particles. The output of this recipe looks like this:

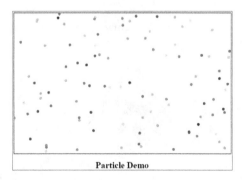

Particle Demo

How to do it...

The recipe is shown here:

The HTML code:

```html
<html>
<head>
<title>Particle demo</title>
<script src="particledemo.js"></script>
</head>
<body onload="init();">
<center>
<canvas id="MyCanvasArea" width="800" height="500" style="border:2px
solid blue;" >
    your browser does not support canvas
</canvas>
<h1>Particle Demo</h1>
</center>
</body>
</html>
```

The JavaScript code:

```javascript
var can;
var ctx;
var particles=[];
var particle;
var part;
var numParticles=100;
var i;
var bounce=-1;
var r,g,b;


function animate()
{
  reqAnimFrame = window.mozRequestAnimationFrame    ||
              window.webkitRequestAnimationFrame ||
              window.msRequestAnimationFrame    ||
              window.oRequestAnimationFrame
              ;
  clear();
  draw();
  update();
```

```
      reqAnimFrame(animate);
}
function init()
{
  var r,g,b;
  can=document.getElementById('MyCanvasArea');
  ctx=can.getContext('2d');
  for(i=0;i<numParticles;i++) {
    r=parseInt(Math.random()*255);
    g=parseInt(Math.random()*255);
    b=parseInt(Math.random()*255);
    particle={x:Math.random()*can.width,
      y:Math.random()*can.height,
      vx:Math.random()*10-5,
      vy:Math.random()*10-5,
      pcolor:'rgb('+r+','+g+','+b+')'
      };
    particles.push(particle);
  }
  animate();
}
function update()
{
  for(i=0;i<numParticles;i++)
  {
          part = particles[i];
          part.x = part.x + part.vx;   //adding the speed
          part.y = part.y + part.vy;   //adding the speed

      //not letting particle go beyond left or right wall
      if(part.x>can.width)
      {
              part.x = can.width;
              part.vx *= bounce;
          }
          else if(part.x<0)
      {
              part.x = 0;
          part.vx = part.vx * bounce;
          }

      //not letting the particle go beyond roof or ceiling
          if(part.y > can.height)
      {
```

```
                      part.y=can.height;
                      part.vy = part.vy * bounce;
              }
              else if(part.y<0)
              {
                      part.y = 0;
                      part.vy = part.vy * bounce;
              }
          }
  }
  function clear()
  {
    ctx.clearRect(0, 0, can.width, can.height);
  }
  function draw()
  {
    var r,g,b;

    for(i=0;i<numParticles;i++)
    {
      part=particles[i];
      ctx.beginPath();
      ctx.fillStyle=part.pcolor;
      ctx.arc(part.x, part.y, 5, 0, Math.PI * 2, false);
      ctx.fill();
    }
  }
```

How it works...

The basic logic is to create an array of particles with some properties. The properties in this recipe for the particles are x and y coordinates, namely the position of the particle and the vx and vy coordinates for velocity, for example providing movement along the x axis and movement along the y axis. Also, there is a property to set a color for each particle.

The `Math.random()` function plays a major role in deciding the position of the particles and also the value of velocity in the x and y directions. Also, the color is random.

The update function ensures that the particles move and do not cross the borders of the canvas. The draw function draws the number of particles as specified as a value of the `numParticles` variable. The clear function clears the canvas. The functions `clear()`, `update()`, and `draw()` are called in this order.

Try the following:

- ▸ Change the number of particles to any number between 2 and 10
- ▸ Change the number of particles to any number above 100 and less than 1000
- ▸ Change the radius of the arc, which is mentioned in the draw() function

Animating a particle fountain

The particles in the previous recipe originate randomly and then move randomly. In this recipe, with a small change, we can give it a fountain effect. This is achieved by changing the origin of all the particles to a single point. One more change is done in the recipe by drawing a barrel. The output of the recipe is shown here:

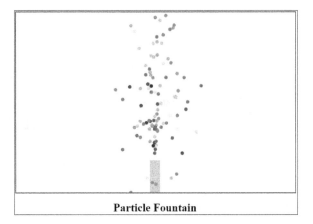

Particle Fountain

How to do it...

The recipe goes as follows:

The HTML code:

```
<html>
<head>
<title>Particle demo</title>
<script src="ParticleFountain.js"></script>
</head>
<body onload="init();">
<center>
```

```
<canvas id="MyCanvasArea" width="800" height="500" style="border:2px
solid blue;" >
   your browser does not support canvas
</canvas>
<h1>Particle Demo</h1>
</center>
</body>
</html>
```

The JavaScript code:

```
var can;
var ctx;
var particles=[];
var particle;
var part;
var numParticles=100;
var i;
var bounce=-1;
var r,g,b;
var gravity=0.4;

function animate()
{
  reqAnimFrame = window.mozRequestAnimationFrame    ||
             window.webkitRequestAnimationFrame ||
             window.msRequestAnimationFrame     ||
             window.oRequestAnimationFrame
             ;
  clear();
  drawBarrel();
  draw();
  update();
  reqAnimFrame(animate);
}
function init()
{
  var r,g,b;
  can=document.getElementById('MyCanvasArea');
  ctx=can.getContext('2d');
  for(i=0;i<numParticles;i++) {
    r=parseInt(Math.random()*255);
    g=parseInt(Math.random()*255);
    b=parseInt(Math.random()*255);
    particle={x:can.width/2,
```

```
        y:can.height-100,
        vx:Math.random()*4-2,
        vy:Math.random()*-14-7,
        pcolor:'rgb('+r+','+g+','+b+')'
        };
      particles.push(particle);
  }
  animate();
}
function update()
{
  for(i=0;i<numParticles;i++)
  {
            part = particles[i];
            part.x = part.x + part.vx;   //adding the speed
            part.y = part.y + part.vy;   //adding the speed

        part.vy+=gravity;

        if(part.x>can.width || part.x<0 || part.y>can.height || part.
y<0)
        {
    part.x=can.width/2;
    part.y=can.height-100;
    part.vx=Math.random()*4-2;
    part.vy=Math.random()*-14-7;
        }
          }
}
function clear()
{
  ctx.clearRect(0, 0, can.width, can.height);
}
function drawBarrel()
{
  ctx.beginPath();
  ctx.fillStyle="rust";
  ctx.fillRect(can.width/2-15,can.height-90,30,100);
  ctx.closePath();
}
function draw()
{
  var r,g,b;
  for(i=0;i<numParticles;i++)
```

```
    {
      part=particles[i];
      ctx.beginPath();
      ctx.fillStyle=part.pcolor;
      ctx.arc(part.x, part.y, 5, 0, Math.PI * 2, false);
      ctx.fill();
    }
  }
}
```

How it works...

The place where all the particles are created is specified and there is one more method named `drawBarrel()` to add to the previous recipe. The other drawing features remain the same.

There's more...

Try the following:

▸   Change the number of particles to `1000` and the radius of a particle to `1`

Animating a rain effect

Rain is a very common but good-to-see animation. In this recipe, the droplets are small lines.

The output looks like this:

Rain

How to do it...

The recipe is as follows:

The HTML code:

```html
<html>
<head>
<title>The Rain</title>
<script src="rain.js"></script>
</head>
<body onload="init();">
<center>
<canvas id="MyCanvasArea" width="800" height="500" style="border:2px
solid blue;" >
   your browser does not support canvas
</canvas>
<h1>Rain</h1>
</center>
</body>
</html>
```

The JavaScript code:

```javascript
var can;
var ctx;
var raindrops=[];
var raindrop;
var part;
var numraindrops=50;
var i;
var bounce=-1;
var r,g,b;

function animate()
{
  reqAnimFrame = window.mozRequestAnimationFrame    ||
              window.webkitRequestAnimationFrame ||
              window.msRequestAnimationFrame     ||
              window.oRequestAnimationFrame
              ;
  clear();
  draw();
  update();
```

```
    reqAnimFrame(animate);
}
function init()
{
  var r,g,b;
  can=document.getElementById('MyCanvasArea');
  ctx=can.getContext('2d');
  r=20;
  g=150;
  b=255;

  for(i=0;i<numraindrops;i++)
  {
    raindrop={x:Math.random()*can.width,
      y:0,
      vy:Math.random()*20+5,
      width:15,
      pcolor:'rgb('+r+','+g+','+b+')'
      };
    raindrops.push(raindrop);
  }

  animate();
}
function update()
{
  for(i=0;i<numraindrops;i++)
  {
          part = raindrops[i];
          part.y = part.y + part.vy;   //adding the speed

      //redraw the drops as soon as the drops cross the bottom
      if(part.y>can.height)
          {
              ctx.beginPath();
              ctx.strokeStyle="blue";//part.pcolor;
              ctx.lineWidth=3;
              part.x=Math.random()*can.width;
              part.y=0;
              ctx.moveTo(part.x,part.y);
              ctx.lineTo(part.x,(part.y+15));
              ctx.stroke();
          }
      }
```

```
}
function clear()
{
   ctx.clearRect(0, 0, can.width, can.height);
}
function draw()
{
   var r,g,b;

   for(i=0;i<numraindrops;i++)
   {
      part=raindrops[i];
      ctx.beginPath();
      ctx.strokeStyle="blue";//part.pcolor;
      ctx.lineWidth=3;
      ctx.moveTo(part.x,part.y);
      ctx.lineTo(part.x,(part.y+15));
      ctx.stroke();
   }
}
```

How it works...

All particles start at *y=0* at the top edge of the canvas, and drop down as the y coordinate changes by the vy factor in the update method. Unlike the drawing of an arc, as in the previous example, here each particle has been drawn as a line. A particle can be of any shape. As soon as the particles touch the bottom, the particles are drawn again. Thus, there is a continuous flow of lines (rain drops).

There's more...

Try the following:

- Change the number of particles
- Change the width of the line

Animating a snow effect

With a little variation, we here a new recipe showing a snow effect:

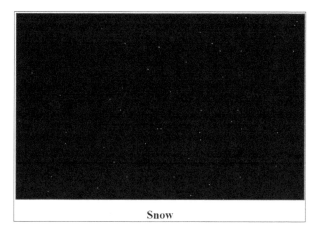

Snow

How to do it...

The recipe is as follows:

The HTML code:

```
<html>
<head>
<title>Snow</title>
<script src="snow.js"></script>
</head>
<body onload="init();">
<center>
<canvas id="MyCanvasArea" width="800" height="500" style="border:2px
solid blue;" >
   your browser does not support canvas
</canvas>
<h1>Snow</h1>
</center>
</body>
</html>
```

The JavaScript code:

```
var can;
var ctx;
var particles=[];
var particle;
var part;
var numParticles=50;
var i;
var bounce=-1;
var r,g,b;

function animate()
{
  reqAnimFrame = window.mozRequestAnimationFrame      ||
                 window.webkitRequestAnimationFrame ||
                 window.msRequestAnimationFrame      ||
                 window.oRequestAnimationFrame
                 ;
  clear();
  draw();
  update();
  reqAnimFrame(animate);
}
function init()
{
  var r,g,b;
  can=document.getElementById('MyCanvasArea');
  ctx=can.getContext('2d');

  for(i=0;i<numParticles;i++) {
    r=255;
    g=255;
    b=255;
    particle={x:Math.random()*can.width,
      y:Math.random()*can.height,
      vx:Math.random()*10-5,
      vy:10,
      pcolor:'rgb('+r+','+g+','+b+')'
      };
    particles.push(particle);
  }
  animate();
}
```

```
function update()
{
  for(i=0;i<numParticles;i++)
  {
            part = particles[i];
            part.y = part.y + part.vy;   //adding the speed

            if(part.y>can.height)
            {
    ctx.beginPath();
    ctx.fillStyle=part.pcolor;
    part.x=Math.random()*can.width;
    part.y=0;
    ctx.arc(part.x, part.y, 1, 0, Math.PI * 2, false);
    ctx.fill();
    ctx.closePath();
            }


        }
}
function clear()
{
  ctx.clearRect(0, 0, can.width, can.height);
}
function draw()
{
  var r,g,b;

  ctx.beginPath();
  ctx.fillStyle="black";
  ctx.fillRect(0,0,can.width,can.height);
        ctx.closePath();

  for(i=0;i<numParticles;i++)
  {
    part=particles[i];
    ctx.fillStyle=part.pcolor;
    ctx.beginPath();
    ctx.fillStyle=part.pcolor;
    ctx.arc(part.x, part.y, 1, 0, Math.PI * 2, false);
    ctx.fill();
  }
}
```

How it works...

This recipe is similar to the rain effect. However, here the particles are circles and white in color. The canvas background is black.

There's more...

Try the following:

- ▶ Change the radius of the circle at both the places in the code
- ▶ Change the number of particles

4

Images and Videos

This chapter introduces how to work on images and videos. It includes the following topics:

- ▸ Drawing and cropping an image
- ▸ Rendering effects to images
- ▸ Drawing a mirror image
- ▸ Clipping a path
- ▸ Animated clipping
- ▸ Converting canvas to image and back to canvas
- ▸ Working with videos
- ▸ Rendering effects to videos
- ▸ Creating a pixelated image focus

Introduction

This chapter focuses on yet another very exciting topic of the HTML5 Canvas, images and videos. Along with providing basic functionality for positioning, sizing, and cropping images and videos, the HTML5 Canvas API also allows us to access and modify the color and transparency of each pixel for both mediums. Let's get started!

Host all the recipes on a web server (I used IIS) as a few recipes will not work on the local `file://protocol`. For security reasons, methods such as `getImageData()` require a web server to function.

Drawing and cropping an image

Let's jump right in by drawing a simple image. In this recipe, you'll learn how to load an image and draw it on the canvas. Also, you will learn to crop an image:

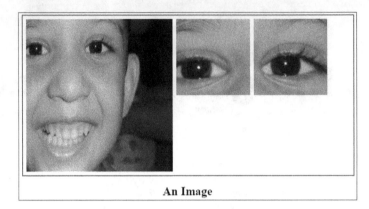

An Image

Follow these steps to draw an image on the canvas.

How to do it

The HTML code to complete this recipe is as follows:

```
<html>
<head>
<title>Image</title>
<script src="ImageDrawing.js"></script>
</head>
<body onload="init();">
<center>
<canvas id="MyCanvasArea" width="900" height="420" style="border:2px
solid blue;" >your browser does not support canvas</canvas>
<h1>An Image</h1>
</center>
</body>
</html>
```

The JavaScript code:

```
var can;
var ctx;
var boyimage;
function init()
```

```
{
  can = document.getElementById('MyCanvasArea'),
  ctx = can.getContext('2d');

  draw();

  function draw()
  {
    boyimage = new Image();
    boyimage.src = 'Images/ohams.png';
    boyimage.onload = function(){
      ctx.drawImage(boyimage, 10, 10,400,400);  //drawing an image
      ctx.drawImage(boyimage, 10, 10,400,400,420,10,200,200); //
      cropped image
      ctx.drawImage(boyimage, 700, 10,400,400,630,10,200,200);//
      cropped image
    }
  }
}
}
```

How it works...

To draw an image, we first need to create an image object using `new Image()`. Note that we've set the `onload` property of the image object before defining the source of the image.

 It's a good practice to define what we want to do with the image when it loads before setting its source. Theoretically, if we were to define the source of the image before we define the onload property, the image could potentially load before the definition is complete (although it's very unlikely).

The key method in this recipe is the `drawImage()` method:

```
context.drawImage(imageObj,destX,destY);
```

Here, `imageObj` is the image object, and `destX` and `destY` are where we want to position the image.

In addition to defining an image position with `destX` and `destY`, we can also add two additional parameters, `destWidth` and `destHeight`, to define the size of our image:

```
context.drawImage(imageObj,destX,destY,destWidth,destHeight);
```

It's a good idea to stay away from resizing an image with the drawImage() method, simply because the quality of the scaled image will be noticeably reduced, similar to the result when we resize an image with the width and height properties of an HTML image element. If image quality is something you're concerned about, it's usually best to work with thumbnail images alongside bigger images if you're creating an application that needs scaled images. If, on the other hand, your application dynamically shrinks and expands images, using the drawImage() method with destWidth and destHeight to scale images is a perfectly acceptable approach.

We can pass an image object and a position to simply draw an image at the given position. We can also pass an image object, a position, and a size to draw an image at the given position with the given size. We can also add six more parameters to the drawImage() method if we want to crop an image:

```
Context.drawImage(imageObj,sourceX,sourceY,sourceWidth,sourceHight,des
tX,destY,destWidth,destHeight);
```

Take a look at the following diagram:

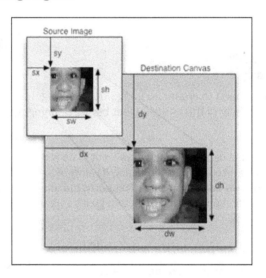

The coordinates sx and sy refer to the top-left corner of the cropped region in the source image. sw and sh refer to the width and height of the cropped image from the source. dx and dy refer to the position of the cropped image on the canvas, and dw and dh refer to the width and height of the resulting cropped image.

The recipe shows both the normal and the cropped image.

Rendering effects to images

This recipe shows the various effects that can be applied to an image. The output of the recipe is as shown here:

Image Effects-normal,negative,gryascale,red,sepia & noise

How to do it

The recipe is as follows:

The HTML code:

```
<html>
<head>
<title>Image</title>
<script src="ImageEffects.js"></script>
</head>
<body onload="init();">
<center>
<canvas id="MyCanvasArea" width="650" height="450" style="border:2px
solid blue;" >
your browser does not support canvas</canvas>
<h1>Image Effects-normal,negative,gryascale,red,sepia& noise</h1>
</center>
</body>
</html>
```

The JavaScript code:

```
var can;var ctx;var boyimage;var x,y;var imageData;var imgPixels;

var red;var green;var blue;var alpha;var avg;

function init(){
  can = document.getElementById('MyCanvasArea'),
  ctx = can.getContext('2d');
  x=10;y=10;
  var imageObj=new Image();
  imageObj.src="goodmorning.jpg";
  imageObj.onload=function(){
    ctx.drawImage(imageObj,x,y,200,200);
    drawInvertedImage();
    drawGrayscaleImage();
    drawRedImage();
    drawSepiaImage();
    drawNoisedImage();
  }
}

function drawInvertedImage(){
  imageData = ctx.getImageData(x, y, can.width,can.height);
  imgPixels = imageData.data;
  for(var i = 0; i<imgPixels.length; i += 4) {
  imgPixels[i] = 255 - imgPixels[i];  // red
  imgPixels[i + 1] = 255 - imgPixels[i + 1];// green
  imgPixels[i + 2] = 255 - imgPixels[i + 2];// blue
      }
  ctx.putImageData(imageData,220,10);
}

function drawGrayscaleImage(){
  imageData = ctx.getImageData(x, y, 200,200);
  imgPixels = imageData.data;

  for(var i = 0; i<imgPixels.length; i += 4) {
  red=imgPixels[i];
  green=imgPixels[i + 1];
  blue=imgPixels[i + 2];
    //alpha=imgPixels[i + 3];
    avg=(red+green+blue)/3;
    imgPixels[i]=avg;
```

```
      imgPixels[i + 1]=avg;
      imgPixels[i + 2]=avg;
      //imgPixels[i + 3]=alpha;
      }
    ctx.putImageData(imageData,430,10);
}

function drawRedImage(){
    imageData = ctx.getImageData(x, y, 200,200);
    imgPixels = imageData.data;

    for(var i = 0; i<imgPixels.length; i += 4) {
    imgPixels[i]=255;
          }
    ctx.putImageData(imageData,10,220);
}
function drawSepiaImage(){

    imageData = ctx.getImageData(x, y, 200,200);
    imgPixels = imageData.data;

    for(var i = 0; i<imgPixels.length; i += 4) {
    red=imgPixels[i];
      green=imgPixels[i + 1];
      blue=imgPixels[i + 2];
      imgPixels[i]=(red * 0.393)+(green * 0.769)+(blue * 0.189);
      imgPixels[i+1]=(red * 0.349)+(green * 0.686)+(blue * 0.168);
      imgPixels[i+2]=(red * 0.272)+(green * 0.534)+(blue * 0.131);
          }
    ctx.putImageData(imageData,220,220);
}
function drawNoisedImage(){
    imageData = ctx.getImageData(x, y, 200,200);
    imgPixels = imageData.data;
var random1;
    var random2;
    var random3;

    for(var i = 0; i<imgPixels.length; i += 4) {
    random1=0.6+Math.random()*0.4;
      random2=0.6+Math.random()*0.4;
      random3=0.6+Math.random()*0.4;
```

```
      imgPixels[i]=imgPixels[i]*random1+10;
      imgPixels[i+1]=imgPixels[i+1]*random2+10;
      imgPixels[i+2]=imgPixels[i+2]*random3-10;
          }
   ctx.putImageData(imageData,430,220);
   }
```

How it works...

Although the code is lengthy, it is not difficult to understand. In the output, you can see a total of five effects on the original image. Five different functions are written to produce these effects. Every pixel is made up of four components: red, green, blue, and alpha. Manipulation of these components applies the relevant effect to the image.

Drawing a mirror image

Everyone knows what a mirror image looks like. So here is the output of our new recipe:

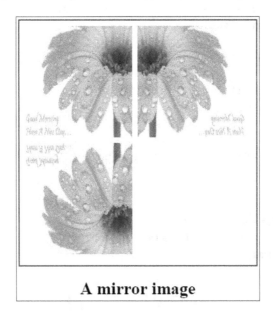

A mirror image

How to do it

The recipe goes as follows:

The HTML code:

```html
<html>
<head>
<title>Image</title>
<script src="MirrorImage.js"></script>
</head>
<body onload="init();">
<center>
<canvas id="MyCanvasArea" width="440" height="440" style="border:2px
solid blue;" > your browser does not support canvas</canvas>
<h1>A mirror image</h1>
</center>
</body>
</html>
```

The JavaScript code:

```javascript
var can;
var ctx;
var flowerimage;
function init()
{
  can = document.getElementById('MyCanvasArea'),
  ctx = can.getContext('2d');

  draw();

  function draw()
  {
    flowerimage = new Image();
    flowerimage.src = 'goodmorning.jpg';
    flowerimage.onload = function(){
      ctx.drawImage(flowerimage,10,10,200,200);
      ctx.save();

      ctx.scale(1,-1);
      ctx.translate(0, -100);
      ctx.drawImage(flowerimage, 10, -320,200,200);
      //drawing an image
```

```
        ctx.restore();

        ctx.scale(-1,1);
        ctx.translate(-100,0);
        ctx.drawImage(flowerimage,-320,10,200,200);
      }
    }
  }
```

How it works...

Scaling, translating, canvas saving, and restoring are used to display the mirror image. Refer to the previous chapter to find out about scaling and translation. The way to draw the image remains the same.

Clipping a path

Clipping an image is the concept of picking a part of the image. The part can be of any shape. In this recipe, I am using a circle. The output of the recipe is as shown here:

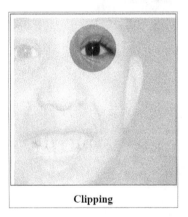

Clipping

How to do it

The following is the code for the recipe:

The HTML code:

```
<html>
<head>
<title>Image</title>
<script src="Clipping.js"></script>
```

```
</head>
<body onload="init();">
<center>
<canvas id="MyCanvasArea" width="500" height="500" style="border:2px
solid blue;" >your browser does not support canvas</canvas>
<h1>Clipping</h1>
</center>
</body>
</html>
```

The JavaScript code:

```
var can;
var ctx;
var boyimage;
var x,y;
var imageData;
var imgPixels;
var clipX,clipY,radius;

function init()
{
  can = document.getElementById('MyCanvasArea'),
  ctx = can.getContext('2d');
  x=10;y=10;

  var imageObj=new Image();

  imageObj.src="ohams.jpg";


  imageObj.onload=function()
  {
    clipX=250;
    clipY=100;
    radius=70;
    ctx.globalAlpha=0.3;
    ctx.drawImage(imageObj,x,y,can.width,can.height);
    ctx.globalCompositeOperation="source-over";
    ctx.globalAlpha=1.0;
    ctx.beginPath();
    ctx.arc(clipX,clipY,radius,0,Math.PI*2,false);
    ctx.clip();
    ctx.drawImage(imageObj,x,y,can.width,can.height);
  }

}
```

The composite operation of `source-over` is used in this recipe. The image is drawn by calling the `drawImage()` function. Then, the composite operation is applied. After this, the arc is created and then the `clip()` function is used, which does the clipping from where the path begins. You can try drawing different paths.

Animated clipping

Animation always adds life. So, we implement the knowledge of animation gained from *Chapter 3, Animations*.

The output can be shown as follows:

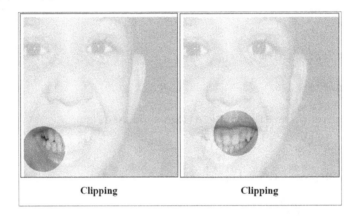

Clipping   Clipping

How to do it

The following is the code for the recipe:

The HTML code:

```html
<html>
<head>
<title>Image</title>
<script src="AnimatedClipping.js"></script>
</head>
<body onload="init();">
<center>
<canvas id="MyCanvasArea" width="500" height="500" style="border:2px
solid blue;" >
    your browser does not support canvas
```

```
</canvas>
<h1>Clipping</h1>
</center>
</body>
</html>
```

The JavaScript code:

```
var can;
var ctx;
var boyimage;
var x,y;
var imageData;
var imgPixels;
var clipX,clipY,radius;
var imageObj;
var xFactor=0;
var bounce=-1;
var clipVX,clipVY;
function init()
{
  can = document.getElementById('MyCanvasArea'),
  ctx = can.getContext('2d');
  x=10;y=10;

  clipX=250;
  clipY=100;
  radius=70;

  imageObj=new Image();

  imageObj.src="ohams.jpg";

  clipVX=Math.random()*10-5;
  clipVY=Math.random()*10-5;

  imageObj.onload=function()
  {
    drawClip();
  }
  animate();
}
function drawClip()
{
```

```
    ctx.save();
    ctx.globalAlpha=0.3;
    ctx.drawImage(imageObj,x,y,can.width,can.height);
    ctx.globalCompositeOperation="source-over";
    ctx.globalAlpha=1.0;
    ctx.beginPath();
    clipX=clipX+xFactor;
    ctx.arc(clipX,clipY,radius,0,Math.PI*2,false);
    ctx.closePath();
    ctx.clip();
    ctx.drawImage(imageObj,x,y,can.width,can.height);
    ctx.restore();
}
function update()
{

    clipX=clipX+clipVX;
    clipY=clipY+clipVY;
    //not letting particle go beyond left or right wall
    if(clipX>can.width)
        {
        clipX = can.width;
        clipVX *= bounce;
            }
else if(clipX<0)
        {
        clipX = 0;
        clipVX = clipVX * bounce;
            }

        //not letting the particle go beyond roof or ceiling
if(clipY>can.height)
        {
        clipY=can.height;
        clipVY = clipVY * bounce;
            }
else if(clipY<0)
            {
            clipY = 0;
            clipVY = clipVY * bounce;
            }

}
```

```
function animate()
{
   reqAnimFrame = window.mozRequestAnimationFrame     ||
                  window.webkitRequestAnimationFrame ||
                  window.msRequestAnimationFrame     ||
                  window.oRequestAnimationFrame
                  ;
   clear();
   drawClip();
   update();
   reqAnimFrame(animate);
}
function clear()
{
   ctx.clearRect(0, 0, can.width, can.height);
}
```

How it works...

We already discussed the animation cycle. The functions for clearing the canvas, updating the clip, and clipping are called in this cycle.

Converting canvas to image and back to canvas

The output of this recipe may not be attractive, but the recipe is definitely useful. Whatever you draw on the canvas can be saved as an image:

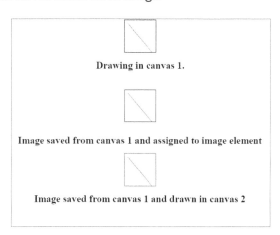

How to do it

The recipe code is as follows:

The HTML code:

```html
<html>
<head>
<title>Image</title>
<style>
img {
border: 1px solid black;
}
</style>
<script src="CanvasToImageAndBackToCanvas.js"></script>
</head>
<body onload="init();">
<center>
<canvas id="MyCanvasArea1" width="100" height="100" style="border:2px
solid blue;" >
your browser does not support canvas
</canvas>
<h1>Drawing in canvas 1.</h1>
<br><br>
<imgsrc="" id="myimg" alt="here goes the image"><br><br>
<h1>Image saved from canvas 1 and assigned to image element</h1>
<canvas id="MyCanvasArea2" width="100" height="100" style="border:2px
solid green;" >
your browser does not support canvas
</canvas>
<h1>Image saved from canvas 1 and drawn in canvas 2</h1>
</center>
</body>
</html>
```

The JavaScript code:

```javascript
var can1;
var ctx1;
var can2;
var ctx2;
function init()
{
  can1 = document.getElementById('MyCanvasArea1');
  ctx1 = can1.getContext('2d');
```

```
    can2=document.getElementById("MyCanvasArea2");
    ctx2=can2.getContext('2d');
    draw();
draw1();
    function draw()
    {

ctx1.beginPath();
    ctx1.moveTo(10,10);
    ctx1.lineTo(130,150);
ctx1.stroke();
    ctx1.closePath();

var dataurl=can1.toDataURL();

    document.getElementById('myimg').src=dataurl;

    var img=new Image();

    img.onload=function(){
      ctx2.drawImage(img,0,0,100,100,0,0,100,100);
      }
    img.src=can1.toDataURL();
    }
}
```

How it works...

In this recipe, the line drawn on the canvas is converted into a data URL. You can display the URL in an alert window just to see how it looks. The data URL is assigned as a source of the image element myimg. This image can then be drawn on another canvas.

Thus, pictures dynamically drawn on a canvas can be saved as images and later can be rendered as an image on another canvas.

Working with videos

In this recipe, you will be introduced to another element of HTML5, `<video>`.

To embed video, we need the video tag, and to work on it, we need the canvas API. The output of this recipe looks like this:

A Video

How to do it

The recipe is as follows:

The HTML code:

```html
<html>
<head>
<title>Video</title>
</head>
<body>
<center>
<video id="myVideo" autoplay="true" loop="true" width=200 height=200>
    <source src="happynewyear.mp4" type="video/mp4"/>
    The browser doesn't support video
</video>
<h1>A Video</h1>
</center>
</body>
</html>
```

How it works...

It's the video tag that does the trick. The video is played in a loop, and there are no controls available to pause or stop the video. If you need to see the controls, add the attribute controls to the video element (`<video controls id="myVideo" …..`).

One important point to remember is that your webserver MIME types should list the type of video you choose to play and the browser should support these. I executed on Google Chrome 4 with the IIS 7 web server to support it. I had to add the file extension `.mp4` and the type `video/mp4` to the list of MIME types. This is available in the options when you open the IIS manager through administrative tools available in the control panel of a Windows system.

Rendering effects to videos

This example is similar to the effects given to the image. Here the video's colors are changed. Here we change the original colors to invert and grayscale. Also, we give it an embossed effect. So, obviously, we will have three different canvases to show three different effects.

The output looks like this:

Video Effects (inverted, grayscale and embossed)

How to do it

The recipe is as follows:

The HTML code:

```
<html>
<head>
<title>Video</title>
<script src="VideoEffects.js"></script>
</head>
```

```html
<body onload="init();">
<center>
<video id="myVideo" autoplay="true" loop="true" width=200 height=200>
    <source src="happynewyear.mp4" type="video/mp4"/>
    The browser doesn't support video
</video>
<canvas id="MyCanvasArea1" width=200 height=300 style="border:2px
solid blue;">browser does not support canvas
</canvas>
<canvas id="MyCanvasArea2" width=200 height=300 style="border:2px
solid blue;">browser does not support canvas
</canvas>
<canvas id="MyCanvasArea3" width=200 height=300 style="border:2px
solid blue;">browser does not support canvas
</canvas>
<h1>Video Effects (inverted, grayscale and embossed)</h1>
</center>
</body>
</html>
```

The JavaScript code:

```javascript
var can1;
var ctx1;
var can2;
var ctx2;
var can3;
var ctx3;
var vid;

function init()
{
  can1 = document.getElementById("MyCanvasArea1");
  ctx1 = can1.getContext("2d");
  can2 = document.getElementById("MyCanvasArea2");
  ctx2 = can2.getContext("2d");
  can3 = document.getElementById("MyCanvasArea3");
  ctx3 = can3.getContext("2d");
  vid = document.getElementById("myVideo");
  animate();
}

function animate()
{
```

```
        reqAnimFrame = window.mozRequestAnimationFrame     ||
                       window.webkitRequestAnimationFrame  ||
                       window.msRequestAnimationFrame      ||
                       window.oRequestAnimationFrame
                       ;
        invert();
        grayscale();
        emboss();
        reqAnimFrame(animate);
}
function invert()
{
    ctx1.drawImage(vid, 0, 0);
    var imageData = ctx1.getImageData(0, 0, can1.width,can1.height);
    var pixels = imageData.data;
    for (var i = 0; i<pixels.length; i += 4)
    {
        pixels[i] = 255 - pixels[i]; // red
        pixels[i + 1] = 255 - pixels[i + 1]; // green
        pixels[i + 2] = 255 - pixels[i + 2]; // blue
        // i+3 is alpha (the fourth element)
    }
    ctx1.putImageData(imageData, 0, 0);
}
function grayscale()
{
    ctx2.drawImage(vid, 0, 0);
    var imageData = ctx2.getImageData(0, 0, can2.width,can2.height);
    var pixels = imageData.data;
    var gray;
    for (var i = 0; i<pixels.length; i += 4)
    {
        gray=(pixels[i]+pixels[i+1]+pixels[i+2])/3;
        pixels[i] = gray
        pixels[i + 1] = gray
        pixels[i + 2] = gray
        // i+3 is alpha (the fourth element)
    }
    ctx2.putImageData(imageData, 0, 0);
}
function emboss()
{
    ctx3.drawImage(vid, 0, 0);
```

```
var imageData = ctx3.getImageData(0, 0, can3.width,can3.height);
var pixels = imageData.data;
var wid=imageData.width;
for (var i = 0; i<pixels.length; i += 4)
{
  if(i%4==3)
    continue;
    pixels[i] = 127 + 2*pixels[i] - pixels[i + 4] - pixels[i
    + wid*4];
}

  ctx3.putImageData(imageData, 0, 0);
}
```

How it works...

Three functions for performing three different effects are used in JavaScript. The animation is done in the same way as before. The important aspect is the manipulation of pixels. You are free to experiment on pixels and discover more about effects.

Creating a pixelated image focus

Here is a fancy way to focus an image. In this recipe, we'll explore the art of image pixelation by looping through an algorithm that reduces the pixelation until it's completely focused:

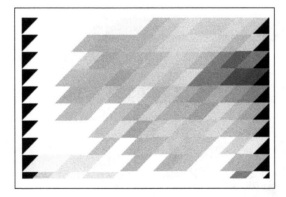

How to do it

The recipe is as follows:

The HTML code:

```html
<html>
<head>
<script src="pixelation.js"></script>
</head>
<body onload="init();">
<canvas id="myCanvas" width="578" height="400"></canvas>
</body>
</html>
```

The JavaScript code:

```javascript
function init()
{
var pixelation = 40;

function focusImage(context, imageObj, sourceWidth, sourceHeight,
destX, destY) {
var sourceX = destX;
var sourceY = destY;

var imageData = context.getImageData(sourceX, sourceY, sourceWidth,
sourceHeight);
var data = imageData.data;

for(var y = 0; y <sourceHeight; y += pixelation) {
for(var x = 0; x <sourceWidth; x += pixelation) {
var red = data[((sourceWidth * y) + x) * 4];
var green = data[((sourceWidth * y) + x) * 4 + 1];
var blue = data[((sourceWidth * y) + x) * 4 + 2];

for(var n = 0; n <pixelation; n++) {
for(var m = 0; m <pixelation; m++) {
if(x + m <sourceWidth) {
data[((sourceWidth * (y + n)) + (x + m)) * 4] = red;
data[((sourceWidth * (y + n)) + (x + m)) * 4 + 1] = green;
data[((sourceWidth * (y + n)) + (x + m)) * 4 + 2] = blue;
}
}
```

```
                    }
                }
            }

            // overwrite original image
context.putImageData(imageData, destX, destY);
pixelation -= 1;
        }
var fps = 20;
        // frames / second
var timeInterval = 1000 / fps;
        // milliseconds
var canvas = document.getElementById('myCanvas');
var context = canvas.getContext('2d');

var imageObj = new Image();
imageObj.onload = function() {
var sourceWidth = imageObj.width;
var sourceHeight = imageObj.height;
var destX = canvas.width / 2 - sourceWidth / 2;
var destY = canvas.height / 2 - sourceHeight / 2;

var intervalId = setInterval(function() {
context.drawImage(imageObj, destX, destY);

if(pixelation< 1) {
clearInterval(intervalId);
            }
else {
focusImage(context, imageObj, sourceWidth, sourceHeight, destX,
destY);
            }

        }, timeInterval);
    };

imageObj.src = 'goodmorning.jpg';
}
```

How it works...

The **pixelation** of an image occurs when the human eye can detect the individual pixels that make up the image. Old-school video game graphics and small images that have been enlarged are good examples of pixelation. Larger the pixels more pixelated the image becomes.

In this recipe, we inspect sample pixels by looking at specific areas in the image based on x, y coordinates. We use the following equations to pick out the RGB component of a pixel based on x, y coordinates:

```
var red = data[((sourceWidth * y) + x) * 4];
var green = data[((sourceWidth * y) + x) * 4 + 1];
var blue = data[((sourceWidth * y) + x) * 4 + 2];
```

With these equations in hand, we render a series of pixelated images over time, where each successive pixelated image is less pixelated than the previous image, until the pixelation value equals 0 and the image is restored to its original state.

5
Interactivity through Events

This chapter introduces how to work on with events. The following topics will be covered:

- ▶ Working with mouse coordinates
- ▶ Making a face smile
- ▶ Detecting a point in a path
- ▶ Simulating car movements
- ▶ Dragging and dropping
- ▶ Combining events and animation
- ▶ Demonstrating a touch event

Introduction

This chapter is one of the most important chapters, as it takes you to the next level of building blocks of application/game development. Everyone loves to interact, and applications or games would be boring if they are more demonstrative than interactive. In this chapter, event handling is introduced. It is one of the most essential parts of any application or game.

Note that, as mentioned in *Chapter 4*, *Images and Videos*, all recipes should be hosted on a local web server for execution. This is because some API functions need a secure environment. In addition, enable the experimental canvas features on your browser. In Chrome, this can be done through `chrome://flags`.

Working with mouse coordinates

This recipe captures one of the mouse events, mousedown, to find which coordinates on the canvas have been clicked. Here is the output:

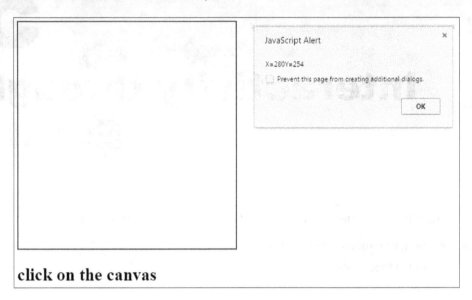

How to do it

The recipe is as follows:

The HTML code is as follows:

```
<html>
<head>
  <title>Mouse Coordinates example</title>
  <script src="mouseCoords.js"></script>
</head>
<body onload=init()>
  <canvas width="400" height="400" id="MyCanvasArea" style="border:2px
  solid blue;">
    Canvas tag is not supported by your browser
  </canvas>
  <br>
  <h1>click on the canvas</h1>
</body>
</html>
```

The JavaScript code is as follows:

```
var ctx;
var can;
function init()
{
  can=document.getElementById("MyCanvasArea");
  ctx=can.getContext("2d");
  can.addEventListener("mousedown",doMouseDown,false);
}
function doMouseDown(event)
{
  xPos=event.pageX;
  yPos=event.pageY;
  alert("X=" + xPos + "Y=" + yPos);
}
```

How it works...

In this example, the focus is on mouse events. The `can.addEventListener("mousedow n",doMouseDown,false)` statement is responsible for registering a listener for the event that a user will perform on the canvas.

Whenever a user clicks (`mousedown`) anywhere inside the canvas, the mouse coordinates are captured and displayed in the alert box. What is to be done on the `mousedown` event is mentioned in the `doMouseDown()` method, which uses the event object to get the coordinates of the position where the click event is performed.

There's more...

Try the following:

- ▸ Do something else on the click of the mouse, such as changing the color of the canvas or displaying a message instead of the mouse coordinates.

Making a face smile

This recipe is another example of handling a mouse event. As soon as you place the cursor on the face, it smiles; otherwise, it shows a sad expression. This is a simple recipe, the output of which looks like this:

How to do it

The recipe is as follows:

The HTML code:

```html
<html>
<head>
  <title>Event Handling example</title>
  <script src="Smiley.js"></script>
</head>
<body onload=init()>
  <h1>I love to smile. Please place the cursor on me</h1>
  <canvas width="400" height="400" id="MyCanvasArea" style="border:2px
  solid blue;">
    Canvas tag is not supported by your browser
  </canvas>
</body>
</html>
```

The JavaScript code:

```javascript
var can;
var ctx;
function init(){
```

```
        can=document.getElementById("MyCanvasArea");
        can.addEventListener('mousemove',function(event){
    if(event.region)
    {
      clear();
      drawSmiley("true");
    }
    else
    {
      clear();
      drawSmiley("false");
    }
  }
  );
  ctx=can.getContext("2d");
  drawSmiley("false");
}
function drawSmiley(status){
  ctx.beginPath();
  xPos=can.width/2;
  yPos=can.height/2;
  drawCircle(ctx,xPos,yPos,100,2,"crimson","yellow");
  ctx.addHitRegion({id: "face"});
  drawCircle(ctx,xPos-40,yPos-40,10,2,"black","black");
  drawCircle(ctx,xPos+40,yPos-40,10,2,"black","black");
  if(status=="true")
    drawArc(ctx,xPos,yPos,60,0,180,false,"black","yellow");
  else if(status=="false")
    drawArc(ctx,xPos,yPos+50,60,0,180,true,"black","yellow");
}
function clear(){
  ctx.clearRect(0,0,can.width,can.height);
}
function drawCircle(ctx,xPos, yPos, radius,borderwidth, borderColor,
fillColor){
      var startAngle =   0 * (Math.PI/180);
      var endAngle   = 360 * (Math.PI/180);

      var radius = radius;

      ctx.strokeStyle = borderColor;
      ctx.fillStyle   = fillColor;
      ctx.lineWidth   = borderwidth;
```

```
            ctx.beginPath();
            ctx.arc(xPos, yPos, radius, startAngle, endAngle, false);
            ctx.fill();
            ctx.stroke();
    }
    function drawArc(ctx,xPos,yPos,radius,startAngle,endAngle,anticlockwis
    e,lineColor, fillColor){
        var startAngle = startAngle * (Math.PI/180);
        var endAngle   = endAngle   * (Math.PI/180);
        var radius = radius;

        ctx.strokeStyle = lineColor;
        ctx.fillStyle   = fillColor;
        ctx.lineWidth   = 2;
        ctx.beginPath();
        ctx.arc(xPos,yPos,radius,startAngle,endAngle,anticlockwise);
        ctx.fill();
        ctx.stroke();
    }
```

How it works...

The `drawArc()` and `drawCircle()` functions have been explained in previous chapters and are easy to understand. We use these for drawing. The most important method in the recipe is the `addHitRegion()` method. Whatever area is drawn before this method is the hit region area. In our recipe, this method is placed just after the drawing of the largest circle (the face). Now, that's the region where, if the cursor is placed there, we change the arc and thereby change the expression and make the face smile.

The `addEventListener()` method ensures that the click of the mouse (`mousedown` event) will be listened to and an appropriate action taken.

There's more...

Try the following:

- Change the color of the smiley
- Make the face wink

Detecting a point in a path

This is another example of a mouse event, but another new concept is introduced here: how to find whether a point lies in a given path. The output of the recipe is as follows:

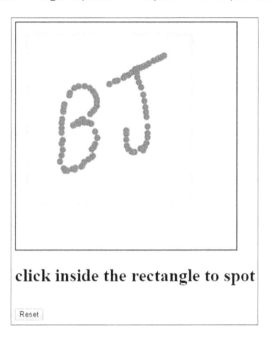

How to do it

The recipe is as follows:

The HTML code:

```
<html>
<head>
  <title>Point In Path Example</title>
  <script src="pointinpath.js"></script>
</head>
<body onload=init()>
  <canvas width="400" height="400" id="MyCanvasArea" style="border:2px
  solid blue;">
    Canvas tag is not supported by your browser
  </canvas>
```

```
      <br>
      <h1>click inside the rectangle to spot</h1>
      <br>
      <form>
        <input type="button" onclick="init();" value="Reset" >
      </form>
  </body>
  </html>
```

The JavaScript code:

```
  var ctx;
  var can;
  function init(){
    can=document.getElementById("MyCanvasArea");
    ctx=can.getContext("2d");
    can.addEventListener("mousedown",doMouseDown,false);
    clear();
    drawRectangle();
  }
  function drawRectangle(){
    ctx.beginPath();
    ctx.strokeStyle="cyan";
    ctx.lineWidth=4;
    ctx.rect(20,20,300,300);
    ctx.stroke();
    ctx.closePath();
  }
  function doMouseDown(event){
    xPos=event.pageX;
    yPos=event.pageY;
    if(ctx.isPointInPath(xPos,yPos))
    {
      //clear();
      drawCircle(xPos,yPos,5,2,"red","green");
      //alert(xPos+","+yPos);
      drawRectangle();
    }
  }
  function clear(){
    ctx.clearRect(0,0,can.width,can.height);
  }
```

```
function drawCircle(xPos, yPos, radius,borderwidth, borderColor,
fillColor){
    var startAngle =    0 * (Math.PI/180);
    var endAngle    = 360 * (Math.PI/180);
    var radius = radius;
    ctx.strokeStyle = borderColor;
    ctx.fillStyle   = fillColor;
    ctx.lineWidth   = borderwidth;
    ctx.beginPath();
    ctx.arc(xPos, yPos, radius, startAngle, endAngle, false);
    ctx.fill();
    ctx.stroke();
    ctx.closePath();
}
```

How it works...

In this new recipe, we introduce the concept of finding a point in a path. The path is defined by the `beginPath()` and `closePath()` methods. So, you need to focus on the `drawRectangle()` method in this recipe. This method contains the code that defines the path. The path is just a rectangle of 300 x 300 starting from the coordinates `x=20` and `y=20`. All the points lying in this path are detected by the `isPointInPath()` method.

A very important point to note is that after drawing the rectangle, if you draw something else, then the path changes. Therefore, in this recipe, the if condition in the event handler (that is, the `doMouseDown()` method) calls the method to draw the rectangle again. This is because, if the mouse is clicked again, then the region has to be the rectangle and not the circle that is drawn just before the call to `drawRectangle()`. In short, the region of points in the path has to be sustained.

There's more...

Try the following:

▸ Comment the call to `drawRectangle()`, which is placed inside the `if` block.

Simulating car movements

This is a very crude recipe to introduce key events. It is a recipe that just gives you a fair idea of how the movements of objects can occur on a key press, which is very useful for gaming. The output is as follows:

How to do it

The recipe is as follows:

The HTML code:

```
<html>
<head>
  <title>Event Handling example</title>
  <script src="CarMoves.js"></script>
</head>
<body onload=init()>
  <canvas width="800" height="800" id="MyCanvasArea" style="border:2px
  solid blue;" tabindex="0">
    Canvas tag is not supported by your browser
  </canvas>
</body>
</html>
```

The JavaScript code:

```
var ctx;
var can;
var xPos;
var yPos;
var rot;
```

```javascript
var carimage;
var TO_RADIANS = Math.PI/180;
function init(){
  can = document.getElementById("MyCanvasArea");
  can.addEventListener('keydown', doKeyDown, true);
  ctx = can.getContext("2d");

  xPos=can.width/2;
  yPos=can.height/2;
  carimage=new Image();
  carimage.src='carTopView.png';
  carimage.onload=function(){
  drawRotatedImage(carimage,xPos,yPos,rot);
  }
  rot=1;
  var TO_RADIANS = Math.PI/180;
  function drawRotatedImage(image, x, y, angle) {
    with(ctx){
      // move to the middle of where we want to draw our image
      translate(x, y);
      // rotate around that point, converting our
      // angle from degrees to radians
      rotate(angle * TO_RADIANS);
      // draw it up and to the left by half the width
      // and height of the image
      drawImage(image, -(image.width/2), -(image.height/2));
    }
  }
  function doKeyDown(e)
  {
    if (e.keyCode == 38) {
      if(yPos>15)
      {
        clear();
        drawRotatedImage(carimage,xPos,yPos--,0);
      }
    }
    else if(e.keyCode == 40)
    {
      if(yPos<can.height)
      {
        clear();
        drawRotatedImage(carimage,xPos,yPos++,0);
      }
```

```
        }
        else if(e.keyCode == 37)
        {
          if(xPos>0)
          {
            clear();
            drawRotatedImage(carimage,xPos,yPos,rot--);
          }
        }
        else if(e.keyCode == 39)
        {
          if(xPos<can.width)
          {
            clear();
            drawRotatedImage(carimage,xPos,yPos,rot++);
          }
        }
      }
      function clear() {
        can.width = can.width;
      }
    }
```

How it works...

In this recipe, there is a single method, doKeyDown(), which is called when you press one of the arrow keys. A more important method here is named drawRotatedImage, which is where we use the concepts of translation and rotation. The translation is done in order to initially bring the image to the center. Later, whenever a key is pressed, the coordinates changes and therefore the point around which the rotation has to be done changes. The point around which the rotation needs to be done is controlled by translation. The angle of the object is changed by applying rotation.

There's more...

Try the following:

- ▶ Comment the call to the translate() method
- ▶ Work with keys such as *W, A ,S*, and *D* to instead of arrow keys

Dragging and dropping

In this recipe, we'll tackle the drag and drop event listeners. Without the Events class or some other lightweight JavaScript library, drag-and-drop operations can be quite cumbersome to develop. We can use `mouseover`, `mousedown`, `mousemove`, `mouseup`, and `mouseout` event listener to handle different phases of the drag-and-drop operation. In this recipe, we use `mousedown`, `mouseup`, and `mousemove`. That's what we require for drag and drop. The output is as follows:

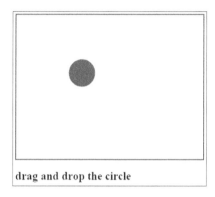

How to do it

The recipe is as follows:

The HTML code:

```
<html>
<head>
<title>Canvas Drag and Drop</title>
<script src="dragdrop.js"></script>
</head>
<body onload=init()>
<section>

<canvas id="MyCanvasArea" width="400" height="300" style="border:2px
solid blue;">
    Canvas tag is not supported by your browser
</canvas>
<h1>drag and drop the circle</h1>
</section>
</body>
</html>
```

The JavaScript code:

```javascript
var can;
var ctx;
var x = 75;
var y = 50;
var WIDTH = 400;
var HEIGHT = 300;
var dragok = false;
function rect(x,y,w,h) {
 ctx.beginPath();
 ctx.rect(x,y,w,h);
 ctx.closePath();
 ctx.fill();
}

function clear() {
 ctx.clearRect(0, 0, WIDTH, HEIGHT);
}
function init() {
 can = document.getElementById("MyCanvasArea");
 ctx = can.getContext("2d");
 can.onmousedown = doMouseDown;
 can.onmouseup = doMouseUp;
 return setInterval(draw, 10);
}
function draw() {
 clear();
 drawCircle(x-15,y-15,30,3,"yellow","purple");
}
function doMouseMove(e){
 if (dragok){
  x = e.pageX - can.offsetLeft;
  y = e.pageY - can.offsetTop;
 }
}
function doMouseDown(e){
 if (e.pageX < x + 15 + can.offsetLeft && e.pageX > x - 15 +
 can.offsetLeft && e.pageY < y + 15 + can.offsetTop &&
 e.pageY > y -15 + can.offsetTop){
  x = e.pageX - can.offsetLeft;
  y = e.pageY - can.offsetTop;
```

```
    dragok = true;
    can.onmousemove = doMouseMove;
   }
  }
}
function doMouseUp(){
 dragok = false;
 can.onmousemove = null;
}
function drawCircle(xPos, yPos, radius,borderwidth, borderColor,
fillColor){
        var startAngle =   0 * (Math.PI/180);
        var endAngle   = 360 * (Math.PI/180);

        var radius = radius;

        ctx.strokeStyle = borderColor;
        ctx.fillStyle   = fillColor;
        ctx.lineWidth   = borderwidth;

        ctx.beginPath();
        ctx.arc(xPos, yPos, radius, startAngle, endAngle, false);
        ctx.fill();
        ctx.stroke();
        ctx.closePath();
}
```

How it works...

Drag and drop is handled in three phases:

1. Detect a mousedown event over a shape, which begins the operation
2. Position the shape according to the mouse coordinates using the mousemove event listener
3. Drop the shape when the mouse button is released (mouseup)

Combining events and animation

This is one of the simplest possible games to start with. It's a recipe that combines events with animation. The output is as follows:

How to do it

The recipe is as follows:

The HTML code:

```
<html>
<head>
  <title>Event Handling example</title>
  <script src="simplegame.js"></script>
</head>
<body onload=animate()>

  <h1>Score Area</h1>
  <canvas width="300" height="100" id="MyScoreArea" style="border:2px
  solid green;" tabindex="0">
    Canvas tag is not supported by your browser
  </canvas>
  <br>
  <h1>click the yellow circle to score</h1>
```

```
<canvas style="background-image:-webkit-canvas(mask);" width="800"
height="500" id="MyCanvasArea" style="border:2px solid blue;"
tabindex="0">
  Canvas tag is not supported by your browser
</canvas>
</body>
</html>
```

The JavaScript code:

```
var can;
var ctx;
var isAnimating=true;
var cd;
var flag=1;
var cd;
var pd;
var x=300;
var y=200;
var hits=0;
var fps = 1; //frames per second
var lastExecution = new Date().getTime();
function animate(){
  reqAnimFrame = window.mozRequestAnimationFrame    ||
            window.webkitRequestAnimationFrame ||
            window.msRequestAnimationFrame     ||
            window.oRequestAnimationFrame
            ;
   var now = new Date().getTime();
  if ((now - lastExecution) > (1000 / fps)){
  //do actual drawing
    drawClock();
  lastExecution = new Date().getTime();
  }
  reqAnimFrame(animate);
}
function drawClock(){
  can=document.getElementById("MyCanvasArea");
  can1=document.getElementById("MyScoreArea");
  ctx1=can1.getContext('2d');

  can.addEventListener('mousedown',calcScore,true);
```

```
        ctx=can.getContext("2d");
        cd=new Date();
        var str=cd.getHours()+":"+cd.getMinutes()+":"+cd.getSeconds();
        ctx.clearRect(0,0,can.width,can.height);
        ctx.font="60px Arial";
        ctx.fillStyle="green";
        ctx.fillText(str,35,90);
        x=Math.random()*can.width;
        y=Math.random()*can.height;
        drawCircle(ctx,x,y,50,2,"crimson","yellow");
        ctx.addHitRegion({id: "face"});
}
function calcScore(){
    if(event.region=="face")
    {
        hits=hits+1;
        var noOfHits="Number of Hits="+hits;
        ctx1.clearRect(0,0,can1.width,can1.height);
        ctx1.font="20px Arial";
        ctx1.fillStyle="brown";
        ctx1.fillText(noOfHits,30,40);
    }
}
function drawCircle(ctx,xPos, yPos, radius,borderwidth, borderColor,
fillColor){
        var startAngle =   0 * (Math.PI/180);
        var endAngle   = 360 * (Math.PI/180);

        var radius = radius;

        ctx.strokeStyle = borderColor;
        ctx.fillStyle   = fillColor;
        ctx.lineWidth   = borderwidth;

        ctx.beginPath();
        ctx.arc(xPos, yPos, radius, startAngle, endAngle, false);
        ctx.fill();
        ctx.stroke();
}
```

How it works...

There are two canvases in the recipe. One of the canvases shows the animation and a digital clock. Another canvas shows the number of times the circle is hit/clicked. The concepts of addHitRegion and eventlistener are repeated here. It's a recipe that has an animation. When the animation happens, the mousedown (click) event is handled.

There's more...

Try the following:

▸ Change the value of FPS

Demonstrating a touch event

This recipe must be tried out on a touch device. The recipe is very simple, and is just to introduce one more type of event, touch. The output looks like this:

How to do it

The recipe is as follows:

The HTML code:

```
<html>
<head>
<title>touch event</title>
<script>
  var can;
  var ctx;
  var color;
  function init()
  {
    can=document.getElementById("MyCanvasArea");
    ctx=can.getContext("2d");
    can.addEventListener("touchstart",doTouchStart,false);
    color="blue";
    drawRectangle();
```

```
    }
    function drawRectangle()
    {
      ctx.beginPath();
      ctx.rect(0,0,can.width,can.height);
      ctx.fillStyle= color;
      ctx.fill();
      ctx.closePath();
    }
    function doTouchStart(event)
    {
      event.preventDefault();
      if(color=="blue")
        color="green";
      else
        color="blue";
      ctx.clearRect(0,0,can.width,can.height);
      drawRectangle();
    }
  </script>
  <body onload=init()>
    <canvas width="400" height="400" id="MyCanvasArea" style="border:2px
    solid blue;">
      Canvas tag is not supported by your browser
    </canvas>
  </body>
```

How it works...

This is just like a mouse event capture. The statement `event.preventDefault()` allows only the touch event to be captured and prevents the default, the mouse event.

The recipe just changes the color of the rectangle from green to blue and blue to green. Of course, it happens when you touch the canvas.

 This example can be executed on your mobile browser (such as Chrome). You need to access the local file through `file:///sdcard/`. The URL will list all the files on the internal storage. Your recipe must exist on the internal storage.

6

Creating Graphs and Charts

This chapter highlights data representation in the form of graphs and charts with the following topics:

- ▶ Drawing the axes
- ▶ Drawing a simple equation
- ▶ Drawing a sinusoidal wave
- ▶ Drawing a line graph
- ▶ Drawing a bar graph
- ▶ Drawing a pie chart

Introduction

Managers make decisions based on the data representations. The data is usually represented in a report form and in the form of graph or charts. The latter representation plays a major role in providing a quick review of the data.

In this chapter, we represent dummy data in the form of graphs and charts.

Drawing the axes

In school days, we all might have used graph paper and drawn a vertical line called the *y* axis and a horizontal line called the *x* axis. Here, in the first recipe of ours, we do only the drawing of axes. Also, we mark the points at equal intervals. The output looks like this:

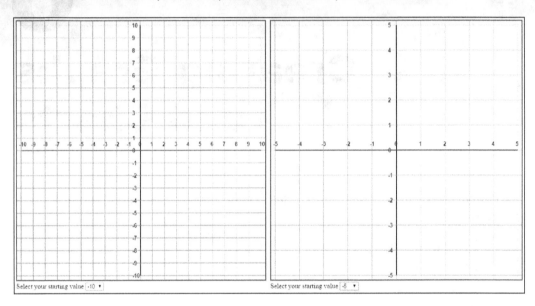

How to do it...

The HTML code is as follows:

```
<html>
<head>
  <title>Axes</title>
  <script src="graphaxes.js"></script>
</head>
<body onload=init()>
  <canvas width="600" height="600" id="MyCanvasArea" style="border:2px
  solid blue;" tabindex="0">
    Canvas tag is not supported by your browser
  </canvas>
  <br>

  <form id="myform">
  Select your starting value
  <select name="startvalue" onclick="init()">
```

```
      <option value=-10>-10</option>
      <option value=-9>-9</option>
      <option value=-8>-8</option>
      <option value=-7>-7</option>
      <option value=-6>-6</option>
      <option value=-5>-5</option>
      <option value=-4>-4</option>
      <option value=-3>-3</option>
      <option value=-2>-2</option>
    </select>
    </form>
  </body>
  </html>
```

The JavaScript code is as follows:

```
var xMin=-10;var yMin=-10;var xMax=10;var yMax=10;
//draw the x-axis
var can;var ctx;var xaxisx;var xaxisy;var yaxisx;var yaxisy;
var interval;var length;
function init(){
  can=document.getElementById('MyCanvasArea');
  ctx=can.getContext('2d');
  ctx.clearRect(0,0,can.width,can.height);
  var sel=document.forms['myform'].elements['startvalue'];
  xMin=sel.value;
  yMin=xMin;
  xMax=-xMin;
  yMax=-xMin;
  drawXAxis();
  drawYAxis();
}
function drawXAxis(){
  //x axis drawing and marking on the same
  xaxisx=10;
  xaxisy=can.height/2;
  ctx.beginPath();
  ctx.lineWidth=2;
  ctx.strokeStyle="black";
  ctx.moveTo(xaxisx,xaxisy);
  xaxisx=can.width-10;
  ctx.lineTo(xaxisx,xaxisy);
  ctx.stroke();
  ctx.closePath();
  length=xaxisx-10;
```

```
      noofxfragments=xMax-xMin;
      interval=length/noofxfragments;
      //mark the x-axis
      xaxisx=10;
      ctx.beginPath();
      ctx.font="bold 10pt Arial";
      for(var i=xMin;i<=xMax;i++)
      {
         ctx.lineWidth=0.15;
         ctx.strokeStyle="grey";
         ctx.fillText(i,xaxisx-5,xaxisy-10);
         ctx.moveTo(xaxisx,xaxisy-(can.width/2));
         ctx.lineTo(xaxisx,(xaxisy+(can.width/2)));
         ctx.stroke();
         xaxisx=Math.round(xaxisx+interval);
      }
      ctx.closePath();
   }
   function drawYAxis(){
      yaxisx=can.width/2;
      yaxisy=can.height-10;
      ctx.beginPath();
      ctx.lineWidth=2;
      ctx.strokeStyle="black";
      ctx.moveTo(yaxisx,yaxisy);
      yaxisy=10
      ctx.lineTo(yaxisx,yaxisy);
      ctx.stroke();
      ctx.closePath();
      yaxisy=can.height-10;
      length=yaxisy-10;
      noofxfragments=yMax-yMin;
      interval=length/noofxfragments;
      //mark the y-axis
      ctx.beginPath();
      ctx.font="bold 10pt Arial";
      for(var i=yMin;i<=yMax;i++)
      {
         ctx.lineWidth=0.15;
         ctx.strokeStyle="grey";
         ctx.fillText(i,yaxisx-20,yaxisy+5);
         ctx.moveTo(yaxisx-(can.height/2),yaxisy);
         ctx.lineTo((yaxisx+(can.height/2)),yaxisy);
         ctx.stroke();
```

```
        yaxisy=Math.round(yaxisy-interval);
    }
    ctx.closePath();
}
```

How it works...

There are two functions in the JavaScript code, namely `drawXAxis` and `drawYAxis`. A canvas is not calibrated the way graph paper is. A simple calculation is used to do this.

In both functions, there are two parts. One part draws the axis and the second marks the axes on regular intervals. These are delimited by `ctx.beginPath()` and `ctx.closePath()`.

In the first part, the canvas width and height are used to draw the axes.

In the second part, we do some calculations. The length of the axis is divided by the number of markers to get the interval. If the starting point is `-3`, then we have `-3`, `-2`, `-1`, `0`, `1`, `2`, and `3` on the axis, which makes 7 marks and 6 parts. The interval is used to generate *x* and *y* coordinate values for the starting point and plot the markers.

There's more...

Try to replace the following:

```
ctx.moveTo(xaxisx,xaxisy-(can.width/2)); (in drawXAxis())
ctx.lineTo(xaxisx,(xaxisy+(can.width/2)));(in drawXAxis())

ctx.moveTo(yaxisx-(can.height/2),yaxisy);(in drawYAxis())
ctx.lineTo((yaxisx+(can.height/2)),yaxisy);(in drawYAxis())
```

With:

```
ctx.moveTo(xaxisx,xaxisy-5);
ctx.lineTo(xaxisx,(xaxisy+5));

ctx.moveTo(yaxisx-5,yaxisy);
ctx.lineTo((yaxisx+5),yaxisy);
```

Also, instead of grey for the markers, you can use red.

Drawing a simple equation

This recipe is a simple line drawing on a graph using an equation. The equation is mentioned and explained in the *How It Works* section. The output looks like this:

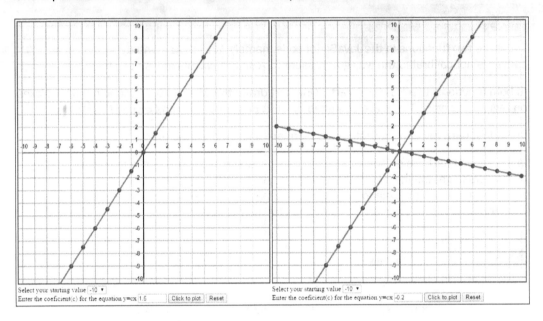

How to do it...

The HTML code is as follows:

```
<html>
<head>
  <title>Equation</title>
  <script src="graphaxes.js"></script>
  <script src="plotequation.js"></script>
</head>
<body onload=init()>
  <canvas width="600" height="600" id="MyCanvasArea" style="border:2px
  solid blue;" tabindex="0">
    Canvas tag is not supported by your browser
  </canvas>
  <br>

  <form id="myform">
  Select your starting value
```

```
<select name="startvalue" onclick="init()">
  <option value=-10>-10</option>
  <option value=-9>-9</option>
  <option value=-8>-8</option>
  <option value=-7>-7</option>
  <option value=-6>-6</option>
  <option value=-5>-5</option>
  <option value=-4>-4</option>
  <option value=-3>-3</option>
  <option value=-2>-2</option>
</select>
<br>
Enter the coeficient(c) for the equation y=cx
<input type="text" size=5 name="coef">
<input type="button" value="Click to plot" onclick="plotEquation()">
<input type="button" value="Reset" onclick="init()">
</form>
</body>
</html>
```

The JavaScript code is as follows:

```
function plotEquation(){
  var coef=document.forms['myform'].elements['coef'];
  var s=document.forms['myform'].elements['startvalue'];
  var c=coef.value;
  var x=parseInt(s.value);
  var xPos; var yPos;
  while(x<=xMax)
  {
    y=c*x;
    xZero=can.width/2;
    yZero=can.height/2;

    if(x!=0)
      xPos=xZero+x*interval;
    else
      xPos=xZero-x*interval;

    if(y!=0)
      yPos=yZero-y*interval;
    else
      yPos=yZero+y*interval;
    ctx.beginPath();
    ctx.fillStyle="blue";
```

```
        ctx.arc(xPos,yPos,5,Math.PI/180,360*Math.PI/180,false);
        ctx.fill();
        ctx.closePath();
        if(x<xMax)
        {
          ctx.beginPath();
          ctx.lineWidth=3;
          ctx.strokeStyle="green";
          ctx.moveTo(xPos,yPos);
          nextX=x+1;
          nextY=c*nextX;
          if(nextX!=0)
            nextXPos=xZero+nextX*interval;
          else
            nextXPos=xZero-nextX*interval;
          if(nextY!=0)
            nextYPos=yZero-nextY*interval;
          else
            nextYPos=yZero+nextY*interval;
          ctx.lineTo(nextXPos,nextYPos);
          ctx.stroke();
          ctx.closePath();
        }
        x=x+1;
      }
    }
```

How it works...

We use one more script in this recipe. There are two scripts referred to by the HTML file. One is the previous recipe named `graphaxes.js`, and the other one is the current one named `plotequation.js`. JavaScript allows you to use the variables created in one file in the other, and this is done in this new recipe. You already know how the axes are drawn.

This recipe is to plot an equation $y=cx$, where c is the coefficient entered by the user. We take the minimum of the x value from the drop-down list and calculate the values for y in a loop. We plot the current and next coordinate and draw a line between the two. This happens until we reach the maximum value of x. Remember that the maximum and minimum value of x and y is same.

There's more...

Try the following:

▶ Input a positive as well as negative value for the coefficient.

Drawing a sinusoidal wave

This recipe also uses the previous recipe of axes drawing. The output looks like this:

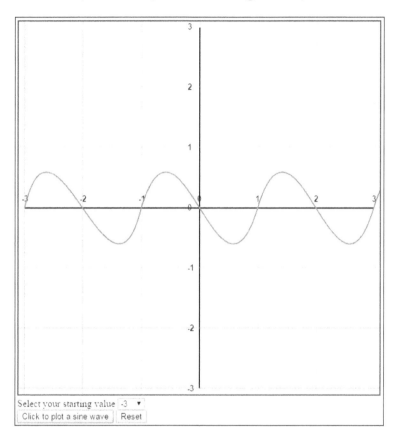

How to do it...

The HTML code is as follows:

```
<html>
<head>
  <title>Equation</title>
  <script src="graphaxes.js"></script>
  <script src="plotSineEquation.js"></script>
</head>
<body onload=init()>
  <canvas width="600" height="600" id="MyCanvasArea" style="border:2px
  solid blue;" tabindex="0">
```

```
    Canvas tag is not supported by your browser
</canvas>
<br>

<form id="myform">
Select your starting value
<select name="startvalue" onclick="init()">
  <option value=-10>-10</option>
  <option value=-9>-9</option>
  <option value=-8>-8</option>
  <option value=-7>-7</option>
  <option value=-6>-6</option>
  <option value=-5>-5</option>
  <option value=-4>-4</option>
  <option value=-3>-3</option>
  <option value=-2>-2</option>
</select>
<br>
<input type="button" value="Click to plot a sine wave"
onclick="plotEquation()">
<input type="button" value="Reset" onclick="init()">
</form>
</body>
</html>
```

The JavaScript code is as follows:

```
functionplotEquation()
{
  var s=document.forms['myform'].elements['startvalue'];
  var x=parseInt(s.value);
  //ctx.fillText(x,100,100);
  var xPos;
  var yPos;
  var noofintervals=Math.round((2*Math.abs(x)+1)/2);
  xPos=10;
  yPos=can.height/2;
  xEnd=xPos+(2*interval);
  yEnd=yPos;
  xCtrl1=xPos+Math.ceil(interval/2);
  yCtrl1=yPos-200;
  xCtrl2=xEnd-Math.ceil(interval/2);
  yCtrl2=yPos+200;
  drawBezierCurve(ctx,xPos,yPos,xCtrl1,yCtrl1,xCtrl2,yCtrl2,
  xEnd,yEnd,"red",2);
```

```
for(var i=1;i<noofintervals;i++)
{
  xPos=xEnd;
  xEnd=xPos+(2*interval);
  xCtrl1=xPos+Math.floor(interval/2)+15;
  xCtrl2=xEnd-Math.floor(interval/2)-15;
  drawBezierCurve(ctx,xPos,yPos,xCtrl1,yCtrl1,xCtrl2,yCtrl2,xEnd,
  yEnd,"red",2);
}
}
function drawBezierCurve(ctx,xstart,ystart,xctrl1,yctrl1,xctrl2,yctrl2
,xend,yend,color,width)
{
  ctx.strokeStyle=color;
  ctx.lineWidth=width;
  ctx.beginPath();
  ctx.moveTo(xstart,ystart);
  ctx.bezierCurveTo(xctrl1,yctrl1,xctrl2,yctrl2,xend,yend);
  ctx.stroke();
}
```

How it works...

We use the Bezier curve to draw the sine wave along the *x* axis. A bit of calculation using the interval between two points, which encompasses a phase, is done to achieve this. The number of intervals is calculated in the following statement:

```
var noofintervals=Math.round((2*Math.abs(x)+1)/2);
```

x is the value in the drop-down list. One phase is initially drawn before the `for` loop begins. The subsequent phases are drawn in the `for` loop. The start and end *x* coordinate changes in every iteration. The ending coordinate for the first sine wave is the first coordinate for the subsequent sine wave.

Drawing a line graph

Graphs are always informative. The basic graphical representation can be a line graph, which is demonstrated here:

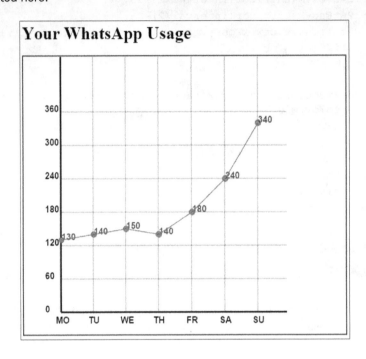

How to do it...

The HTML code is as follows:

```
<html>
<head>
  <title>A simple Line chart</title>
  <script src="linechart.js"></script>
</head>
<body onload=init()>
  <h1>Your WhatsApp Usage</h1>
  <canvas width="600" height="500" id="MyCanvasArea" style="border:2px
  solid blue;" tabindex="0">
    Canvas tag is not supported by your browser
  </canvas>
</body>
</html>
```

The JavaScript code is as follows:

```javascript
function init() {
  var gCanvas = document.getElementById('MyCanvasArea');
  // Ensure that the element is available within the DOM
  var ctx = gCanvas.getContext('2d');
  // Bar chart data
  var data = new Array(7);
  data[0] = "1,130";    data[1] = "2,140";    data[2] = "3,150";
  data[3] = "4,140";
  data[4] = "5,180";  data[5] = "6,240";  data[6] = "7,340";
  // Draw the bar chart
  drawLineGraph(ctx, data, 70, 100, (gCanvas.height - 40), 50);
}
function drawLineGraph(ctx, data, startX, barWidth, chartHeight,
markDataIncrementsIn) {
  // Draw the x axis
ctx.lineWidth = "3.0";
var max=0;
var startY = chartHeight;
drawLine(ctx, startX, startY, startX, 1);
drawLine(ctx, startX, startY, 490, startY);
for(var i=0,m=0;i<data.length;i++,m+=60)
  {
  ctx.lineWidth=0.3;
  drawLine(ctx,startX,startY-m,490,startY-m)
  ctx.font="bold 12pt Arial";
  ctx.fillText(m,startX-30,startY-m);
  }
for(var i=0,m=0;i<data.length;i++,m+=61)
  {
  ctx.lineWidth=0.3;
  drawLine(ctx, startX+m, startY, startX+m, 1);
  var values=data[i].split(",");
  var day;
  switch(values[0])
  {
    case "1":
      day="MO";
      break;
    case "2":
      day="TU";
      break;
    case "3":
```

```
            day="WE";
            break;
        case "4":
            day="TH";
            break;
        case "5":
            day="FR";
            break;
        case "6":
            day="SA";
            break;
        case "7":
            day="SU";
            break;
    }
    ctx.fillText(day,startX+m-10, startY+20);
    }
    //plot the points and draw lines between them
var startAngle =    0 * (Math.PI/180);
var endAngle    = 360 * (Math.PI/180);
var newValues;
for(var i=0,m=0;i<data.length;i++,m+=60)
    {
    ctx.beginPath();

    var values=data[i].split(",");
    var xPos=startX+parseInt(values[0])+m;
    var yPos=chartHeight-parseInt(values[1]);
    ctx.arc(xPos, yPos, 5, startAngle,endAngle, false);
    ctx.fillStyle="red";
    ctx.fill();
    ctx.fillStyle="blue";
    ctx.fillText(values[1],xPos, yPos);
    ctx.stroke();
    ctx.closePath();
    if(i>0){
        ctx.strokeStyle="green";
        ctx.lineWidth=1.5;
        ctx.moveTo(oldxPos,oldyPos);
        ctx.lineTo(xPos,yPos);
        ctx.stroke();
    }
```

```
    oldxPos=xPos;
    oldyPos=yPos;
  }
  }
  function drawLine(ctx, startx, starty, endx, endy) {
  ctx.beginPath();
  ctx.moveTo(startx, starty);
  ctx.lineTo(endx, endy);
  ctx.closePath();
  ctx.stroke();
  }
```

How it works...

All the graphs in the subsequent recipes use an array named **data**. The array element has two parts: one indicates the day and the second indicates the usage in minutes. A split function down the code splits the element into two independent elements.

The coordinates are calculated using a parameter named *m*, which is used in calculating the value of the *x* coordinate. The value in minutes and the chart height is used to calculate the position of *y* coordinate.

Inside the loop, there are two coordinates, which are used to draw a line. One is in the moveTo() method and the other is in the lineTo() method. However, the coordinates oldxPos and oldyPos are not calculated in the first iteration, for the simple reason that we cannot draw a line with a single coordinate. From the next iteration onwards, we have two coordinates and then the line is drawn between the prior and current coordinates.

There's more...

Try the following:

▶   Use your own data.

Drawing a bar graph

Another typical representation, which is widely used, is the bar graph. Here is an output of this recipe:

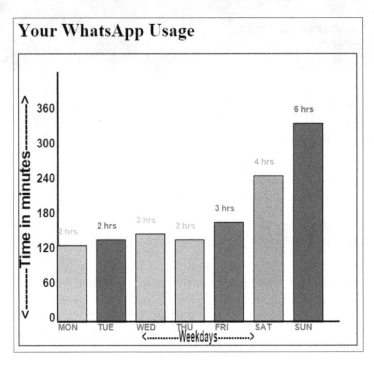

How to do it...

The HTML code is as follows:

```
<html>
<head>
  <title>A simple Bar chart</title>
  <script src="bargraph.js"></script>
</head>
<body onload=init()>
  <h1>Your WhatsApp Usage</h1>
  <canvas width="600" height="500" id="MyCanvasArea" style="border:2px
  solid blue;" tabindex="0">
    Canvas tag is not supported by your browser
  </canvas>
</body>
</html>
```

The JavaScript code is as follows:

```
function init(){
  var gCanvas = document.getElementById('MyCanvasArea');
  // Ensure that the element is available within the DOM
  var ctx = gCanvas.getContext('2d');
  // Bar chart data
  var data = new Array(7);
  data[0] = "MON,130";    data[1] = "TUE,140";    data[2] = "WED,150";
  data[3] = "THU,140";    data[4] = "FRI,170";  data[5] = "SAT,250";
  data[6] = "SUN,340";

  // Draw the bar chart
  drawBarChart(ctx, data, 70, 100, (gCanvas.height - 40), 50);
}
function drawBarChart(ctx, data, startX, barWidth, chartHeight,
markDataIncrementsIn) {
  // Draw the x and y axes
ctx.lineWidth = "3.0";
var startY = chartHeight;
  //drawLine(ctx, startX, startY, startX, 30);
drawBarGraph(ctx, startX, startY, startX, 30,data,chartHeight);
drawLine(ctx, startX, startY, 570, startY);
}

function drawLine(ctx, startx, starty, endx, endy) {
ctx.beginPath();
ctx.moveTo(startx, starty);
ctx.lineTo(endx, endy);
ctx.closePath();
ctx.stroke();
}

function drawBarGraph(ctx, startx, starty, endx,
endy,data,chartHeight) {
ctx.beginPath();
ctx.moveTo(startx, starty);
ctx.lineTo(endx, endy);
ctx.closePath();
ctx.stroke();
var max=0;
  //code to label x-axis
for(i=0;i<data.length;i++)
  {
```

```
      var xValues=data[i].split(",");
      var xName=xValues[0];
      ctx.textAlign="left";
      ctx.fillStyle="#b90000";
      ctx.font="bold 15px Arial";
      ctx.fillText(xName,startx+i*50+i*20,chartHeight+15,200);
      var height=parseInt(xValues[1]);
      if(parseInt(height)>parseInt(max))
        max=height;
      var color='#'+Math.floor(Math.random()*16777215).toString(16);
      drawBar(ctx,startx+i*50+i*20,(chartHeight-height),height,50,color);
      ctx.fillText(Math.round(height/60)+" hrs",startx+i*50+i*20,
      (chartHeight-height-20),200);
      }
    //title the x-axis
ctx.beginPath();
ctx.fillStyle="black";
ctx.font="bolder 20pt Arial";
ctx.fillText("<------------Weekdays------------->",startx+150,chartHei
ght+35,200);
ctx.closePath();


   //y-axis labelling
var ylabels=Math.ceil(max/60);
var yvalue=0;
ctx.font="bold 15pt Arial";
for(i=0;i<=ylabels;i++)
    {
    ctx.textAlign="right";
    ctx.fillText(yvalue,startx-5,(chartHeight-yvalue),50);
    yvalue+=60;
    }
    //title the y-axis
ctx.beginPath();
ctx.font = 'bolder 20pt Arial';
ctx.save();
ctx.translate(20,70);
ctx.rotate(-0.5*Math.PI);
var rText = 'Rotated Text';
ctx.fillText("<--------Time in minutes--------->" , 0, 0);
ctx.closePath();
ctx.restore();
```

```
}
function drawBar(ctx,xPos,yPos,height,width,color){
  ctx.beginPath();
  ctx.fillStyle=color;
  ctx.rect(xPos,yPos,width,height);
  ctx.closePath();
  ctx.stroke();
  ctx.fill();
}
```

How it works...

The processing is similar to that of a line graph, except that here there are rectangles drawn, which represent bars. Also, the numbers 1, 2, 3... represent the day of the week (for example, 1 means Monday).

This line in the code is used to generate random colors for the bars:

```
var color='#'+Math.floor(Math.random()*16777215).toString(16);
```

The number 16777215 is a decimal value for #FFFFF.

Note that the value of the control variable *i* is not directly used for drawing the bar. Rather *i* is manipulated to get the correct coordinates on the canvas and then the bar is drawn using the drawBar() function.

```
drawBar(ctx,startx+i*50+i*20,(chartHeight-
height),height,50,color);
```

There's more...

Try the following:

▶ Use your own data and change the colors.

Drawing a pie chart

A share can be easily represented in form of a pie chart. This recipe demonstrates a pie chart:

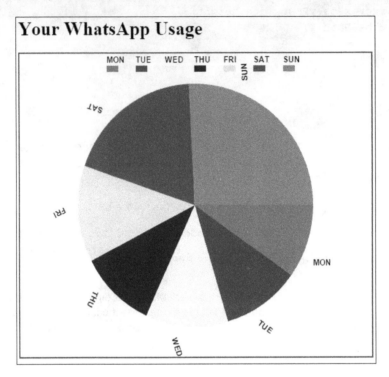

How to do it...

The HTML code is as follows:

```
<html>
<head>
  <title>A simple Pie chart</title>
  <script src="piechart.js"></script>
</head>
<body onload=init()>
  <h1>Your WhatsApp Usage</h1>
  <canvas width="600" height="500" id="MyCanvasArea" style="border:2px
  solid blue;" tabindex="0">
    Canvas tag is not supported by your browser
  </canvas>
</body>
</html>
```

The JavaScript code is as follows:

```
function init()
{
  var can = document.getElementById('MyCanvasArea');
  var ctx = can.getContext('2d');
  var data = [130,140,150,140,170,250,340];
  var colors = ["crimson", "blue", "yellow", "navy", "aqua", "purple",
  "red"];
  var names=["MON","TUE","WED","THU","FRI","SAT","SUN"];
  var centerX=can.width/2;
  var centerY=can.height/2;
  //var center = [can.width/2,can.height / 2];
  var radius = (Math.min(can.width,can.height) / 2)-50;
  var startAngle=0, total=0;
  for(var i in data) {
    total += data[i];
  }
  var incrFactor=-(centerX-centerX/2);
  var angle=0;
  for (var i = 0; i<data.length; i++){
    ctx.fillStyle = colors[i];
    ctx.beginPath();
    ctx.moveTo(centerX,centerY);
    ctx.arc(centerX,centerY,radius,
    startAngle,startAngle+(Math.PI*2*(data[i]/total)),false);
    ctx.lineTo(centerX,centerY);
    ctx.rect(centerX+incrFactor,20,20,10);
    ctx.fill();
    ctx.fillStyle="black";
    ctx.font="bold 10pt Arial";
    ctx.fillText(names[i],centerX+incrFactor,15);
    ctx.save();
    ctx.translate(centerX,centerY);
    ctx.rotate(startAngle);
    var dx=Math.floor(can.width*0.5)-100;
    var dy=Math.floor(can.height*0.20);
    ctx.fillText(names[i],dx,dy);
    ctx.restore();
    startAngle += Math.PI*2*(data[i]/total);
    incrFactor+=50;
  }
}
```

How it works...

Again, the data here is the same, but instead of bars, we use arcs here. The trick is done by changing the end angle as per the data available. Translation and rotation helps in naming the weekdays for the pie chart.

There's more...

Try the following:

▶ Use your own data and change the colors to get acquainted.

7

3D Modeling

This chapter highlights how to represent data in the form of graphs and charts. In this chapter, we will cover:

- ▸ Rendering 3D objects
- ▸ Drawing 3D cubes
- ▸ Drawing a 3D cylinder and a cone
- ▸ Drawing a 3D sphere and a torus
- ▸ Drawing 3D text decorated by particles
- ▸ Drawing a panorama
- ▸ Drawing a snowman

Introduction

One of the libraries is OpenGL **ES** (a library meant especially for **embedded systems**) whose root is **OpenGL** (**Open Graphics Library**). But OpenGL ES is of no use on the web. Therefore, a new API was developed by the Khronos group named **WebGL** (**Web Graphics Library**).

The parent of WebGL happens to be OpenGL ES, whose root is OpenGL. Using OpenGL ES or OpenGL on the web will be difficult as one has to again develop a library especially for the web and then use it for rendering graphics. WebGL is one such library for rendering 2D and 3D graphics on any compatible browser. **three.js** is customized only for 3D graphics.

three.js is a lightweight library based on WebGL for rendering 3D objects on the web. It's a library with a very low level of complexity. The library is still evolving and getting better. This chapter is an effort toward understanding the use of the three.js API with HTML5 Canvas especially for rendering 3D objects.

Please note that the chapter covers the use of three.js and not the explanation. There are many examples and API documentation available at http://threejs.org/ for reference.

Rendering 3D objects

Before we begin with our first recipe, let me introduce two methods that are very important in rendering a 3D object on a canvas. One is `WebGLRenderer()` and the second is `CanvasRenderer()`. The latter renders a scene on the canvas using Canvas 2D Context, and the former does the same using WebGL. Performance-wise, WebGL is better than `CanvasRenderer`. WebGL is, however, device dependent.

The first recipe is a simple display of rotating objects and the output is as follows:

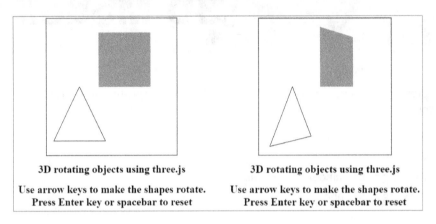

3D rotating objects using three.js

Use arrow keys to make the shapes rotate.
Press Enter key or spacebar to reset

3D rotating objects using three.js

Use arrow keys to make the shapes rotate.
Press Enter key or spacebar to reset

How to do it...

The recipe is as follows:

The HTML code:

```html
<html>
<head>
<title>Rotating Shapes</title>
<script src="../threeLib/build/three.min.js"></script>
<script src="rotatingshapes.js">
</script>
</head>
<body onload="init()">
  <center>
  <canvas width="400" height="400" id="MyCanvasArea" style="border:2px
  solid blue;">
    Canvas tag is not supported by your browser
  </canvas>
```

```
<h1>3D rotating objects using three.js</h1>
<h1>Use arrow keys to make the shapes rotate.<br>
Press Enter key or spacebar to reset</h1>
</center>
</body>
</html>
```

The JavaScript code:

```
var can;
var scene;
var camera;
var renderer;
var triangle;
var square;
var rotX=0;
var rotY=0;
function init() {
    can=document.getElementById("MyCanvasArea");

    renderer = new THREE.WebGLRenderer({
    canvas: can,
    antialias: true    //for smooth effect
    });
    scene = new THREE.Scene();

    camera = new THREE.PerspectiveCamera(
            35,                    // Field of view(FOV)
            can.width / can.height,    // Aspect ratio
            0.1,                   // Near plane(near)
            10000                  // Far plane(far)
     );

    camera.position.z=20;
    camera.lookAt( scene.position );
    draw3DTriangle();
    draw3DSquare();
    renderer.setClearColor( 0xFFFFFF, 1);
    render();
    document.addEventListener("keydown", doKey, false);
}
function render()
```

```
{
  renderer.render(scene,camera);
}
function draw3DTriangle()
{
  var lineGeometry = new THREE.Geometry();

  //vertices for a triangle
  lineGeometry.vertices.push( new THREE.Vector3(-2,-2,0) );
  lineGeometry.vertices.push( new THREE.Vector3(2,-2,0) );
  lineGeometry.vertices.push( new THREE.Vector3(0,2,0) );
  lineGeometry.vertices.push( new THREE.Vector3(-2,-2,0) );

  var material = new THREE.LineBasicMaterial({
      linewidth: 1,
      color: 0x000000
  });

  triangle = new THREE.Line( lineGeometry, material);
  triangle.rotation.set(rotX,rotY,0);
  triangle.position.set(-2.5,-2,4);
  scene.add(triangle);
}

function draw3DSquare()
{
  //another geometry
  var squareGeometry=new THREE.Geometry();
  squareGeometry.vertices.push(new THREE.Vector3(-2,  2, 0));
        squareGeometry.vertices.push(new THREE.Vector3( 2,  2, 0));
        squareGeometry.vertices.push(new THREE.Vector3( 2, -2, 0));
        squareGeometry.vertices.push(new THREE.Vector3(-2, -2, 0));
        squareGeometry.faces.push(new THREE.Face3(0, 1, 2));
        squareGeometry.faces.push(new THREE.Face3(0, 2, 3));
  var squareMaterial = new THREE.MeshBasicMaterial({
                    color:0x8080FF,
                    side:THREE.DoubleSide
                });
  square = new THREE.Mesh(squareGeometry, squareMaterial);
  square.rotation.set(rotX,rotY,0);
        square.position.set(1, 2.0, 4.0);
        scene.add(square);
}
```

```
function doKey(evt) {
    var rotationChanged = true;
    switch (evt.keyCode) {
        case 37: rotY -= 0.04; break;          // left arrow
        case 39: rotY +=  0.04; break;          // right arrow
        case 38: rotX -= 0.04; break;          // up arrow
        case 40: rotX += 0.04; break;          // down arrow
        case 13: rotX = rotY = 0; break;       // return(Enter key)
        case 32: rotX = rotY = 0; break;    //spacebar
        default: rotationChanged = false;
    }
    if (rotationChanged) {
        triangle.rotation.set(rotX,rotY,0);
        square.rotation.set(rotX,rotY,0);
        render();
        evt.preventDefault();
    }
}
```

How it works...

It is simple to draw using the three.js API. You need to create a scene, have a camera positioned on the scene to view it, add the drawings to the scene, and then render the scene and camera on the canvas. Rendering is done using `WebGLRenderer` or `CanvasRenderer`. This recipe uses `WebGLRenderer`. There are two methods to draw two different objects. The methods are `draw3DTriangle()` and `draw3DSquare()` to draw the shapes. There is a `doKey` method to rotate the objects on key press.

It is very important to know the 3D concepts to understand and implement the recipes. 3D concepts are out of the scope of this book; however the recipes are easy to understand and implement.

There's more...

Try:

▶ Animating the rotation of the objects without handling the key event

Drawing 3D cubes

When you hear the word *3D*, the first shape that is visualized is a cube. Without a cube, the concept of 3D drawing is incomplete. So, here is a recipe on cubes. This recipe is a demonstration of four cubes: the first with multicolored faces, the second with a wireframe, the third with the same texture on each face, and the fourth with different textures on each face. The output looks as follows:

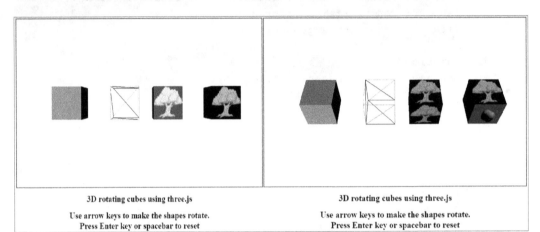

3D rotating cubes using three.js

Use arrow keys to make the shapes rotate.
Press Enter key or spacebar to reset

3D rotating cubes using three.js

Use arrow keys to make the shapes rotate.
Press Enter key or spacebar to reset

How to do it...

The HTML code:

```
<html>
<head>
<title>Cubes</title>
<script src="../threeLib/build/three.min.js"></script>
<script src="cubes.js">

</script>
</head>
<body onload="init()">
  <center>
  <canvas width="1000" height="600" id="MyCanvasArea"
  style="border:2px solid blue;" tabindex="0">
    Canvas tag is not supported by your browser
  </canvas>
  <h1>3D rotating cubes using three.js</h1>
  <h1>Use arrow keys to make the shapes rotate.<br>
```

```
    Press Enter key or spacebar to reset</h1>
    </center>
</body>
</html>
```

The JavaScript code within `cubes.js`:

```
var can;
var scene;
var camera;
var renderer;
var cylinder;
var cube1,cube2,cube3,cube4;
var texture,tmaterial;
var rotX=0;
var rotY=0;
function init() {
    can=document.getElementById("MyCanvasArea");

    renderer = new THREE.WebGLRenderer({
      canvas: can,
      antialias: true     //for smooth effect
    });
    scene = new THREE.Scene();

    camera = new THREE.PerspectiveCamera(
            35,                      // Field of view(FOV)
            can.width / can.height,    // Aspect ratio
            0.1,                     // Near plane(near)
            10000                    // Far plane(far)
     );

    camera.position.z=20;
    camera.lookAt( scene.position );
    renderer.setClearColor( 0xFFFFFF, 1);

    var light = new THREE.DirectionalLight(); // default white light
    light.position.set( 0, 0, 1 );
    scene.add(light);

    draw3DCube();
    draw3DCubeWireFrame();
    draw3DCubeTextured();
```

```
        draw3DCubeTextureMultiFaced();
        render();
        document.addEventListener("keydown", doKey, false);
}
function render()
{
    renderer.render(scene,camera);
}
function draw3DCube()
{
    var cubeGeometry = new THREE.CubeGeometry(2,2,2);
    var material = new THREE.MeshFaceMaterial( [
        new THREE.MeshPhongMaterial( { color: "cyan" } ),
        new THREE.MeshPhongMaterial( { color: "orange" } ),
        new THREE.MeshPhongMaterial( { color: "aqua" } ),
        new THREE.MeshPhongMaterial( { color: "pink" } ),
        new THREE.MeshPhongMaterial( { color: "crimson" } ),
        new THREE.MeshPhongMaterial( { color: "lightyellow" } )
    ] );
    cube1 = new THREE.Mesh(cubeGeometry,material);
    cube1.rotation.set(rotX,rotY,0);
    cube1.position.set(-5,0,3);
    scene.add(cube1);
}

function draw3DCubeWireFrame()
{
    var cubeGeometry=new THREE.CubeGeometry(2,2,2);

    var material = new THREE.MeshLambertMaterial({
                    color:0xFF8000,wireframe:true
                });
    cube2 = new THREE.Mesh(cubeGeometry, material);
    cube2.rotation.set(rotX,rotY,0);
        cube2.position.set(-1, 0, 3);
        scene.add(cube2);
}

function draw3DCubeTextured()
{
    var texture = THREE.ImageUtils.loadTexture('tree4.png');
    texture.needsUpdate = true;
```

```
        var material = new THREE.MeshPhongMaterial( { map: texture,
        transparent: true } );

        var geometry = new THREE.CubeGeometry( 2, 2, 2);

        cube3 = new THREE.Mesh(geometry, material );
        cube3.dynamic=true;
        cube3.position.set(2,0,3);
        scene.add( cube3 );
}

function draw3DCubeTextureMultiFaced()
{
  var materials = [
    new THREE.MeshLambertMaterial({
        ambient: 0xffffff,
        map: THREE.ImageUtils.loadTexture( 'greycapsule.png' ) }),
    new THREE.MeshLambertMaterial({
        ambient: 0xffffff,
        map: THREE.ImageUtils.loadTexture( 'tree4.png' ) }),
    new THREE.MeshLambertMaterial({
        ambient: 0xffffff,
        map: THREE.ImageUtils.loadTexture( 'tree3.jpg' ) }),
    new THREE.MeshLambertMaterial({
        ambient: 0xffffff,
        map: THREE.ImageUtils.loadTexture( 'greycapsule.png' ) }),
    new THREE.MeshLambertMaterial({
        ambient: 0xffffff,
        map: THREE.ImageUtils.loadTexture( 'tree4.png' ) }),
    new THREE.MeshLambertMaterial( {
        ambient: 0xffffff,
        map: THREE.ImageUtils.loadTexture( 'tree3.jpg' ) })
  ];

  var geometry = new THREE.CubeGeometry(2, 2, 2);
  cube4= new THREE.Mesh( geometry, new THREE.MeshFaceMaterial
  (materials) );
  cube4.position.set( 6, 0, 3 );
  scene.add( cube4 );
}

function doKey(evt) {
    var rotationChanged = true;
```

```
switch (evt.keyCode) {
    case 37: rotY -= 0.04; break;          // left arrow
    case 39: rotY +=  0.04; break;         // right arrow
    case 38: rotX -= 0.04; break;          // up arrow
    case 40: rotX += 0.04; break;          // down arrow
    case 13: rotX = rotY = 0; break;       // return(Enter key)
    case 32: rotX = rotY = 0; break;     //spacebar
    default: rotationChanged = false;
}
if (rotationChanged) {
    cube1.rotation.set(rotX,rotY,0);
    cube2.rotation.set(rotX,rotY,0);
    cube3.rotation.set(rotX,rotY,0);
    cube4.rotation.set(rotX,rotY,0);
    render();
    evt.preventDefault();
}
}
```

How it works...

The setup of scene, camera, and rendering is the same as in the previous recipe. What differs is what we want to draw. Here, the methods draw3DCube(), draw3DCubeWireFrame(), draw3DCubeTextured(), and draw3DCubeTexturedMultifaced are used to draw the four different cubes. They are drawn and added to the scene before rendering.

Every method has a way to draw the object. We create a material, design the geometry, add the material to the geometry to create the object, and then add the object to the scene. Here the method used to create the geometry is CubeGeometry(). For the material, the method used is MeshPhongMaterial(). You need to study the API in order to understand the usage of these methods. In the following recipes you will encounter similar methods.

There's more...

Try:

▶ Rendering the scene using CanvasRenderer

Drawing a 3D cylinder and a cone

The method adopted for drawing is more or less the same in each of the recipes. This recipe shows some more shapes. The output is as follows:

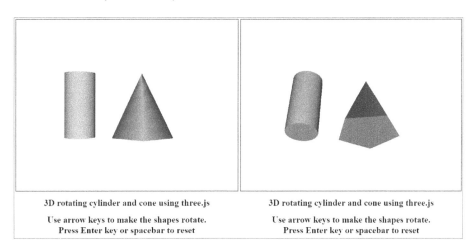

3D rotating cylinder and cone using three.js

Use arrow keys to make the shapes rotate.
Press Enter key or spacebar to reset

3D rotating cylinder and cone using three.js

Use arrow keys to make the shapes rotate.
Press Enter key or spacebar to reset

How to do it...

The HTML code:

```
<html>
<head>
<title>Cylinders</title>
<script src="../threeLib/build/three.min.js"></script>
<script src="cylinders.js">

</script>
</head>
<body onload="init()">
  <center>
  <canvas width="800" height="600" id="MyCanvasArea" style="border:2px
  solid blue;" tabindex="0">
    Canvas tag is not supported by your browser
  </canvas>
  <h1>3D rotating cylinder and cone using three.js</h1>
  <h1>Use arrow keys to make the shapes rotate.<br>
  Press Enter key or spacebar to reset</h1>
  </center>
</body>
</html>
```

The JavaScript code:

```javascript
var can;
var scene;
var camera;
var renderer;
var cylinder;
var cone;
var rotX=0;
var rotY=0;
function init() {
    can=document.getElementById("MyCanvasArea");

    renderer = new THREE.WebGLRenderer({
    canvas: can,
    antialias: true     //for smooth effect
    });
    scene = new THREE.Scene();

    camera = new THREE.PerspectiveCamera(
            35,                      // Field of view(FOV)
            can.width / can.height,     // Aspect ratio
            0.1,                     // Near plane(near)
            10000                    // Far plane(far)
      );

    camera.position.z=20;
    camera.lookAt( scene.position );
    draw3DCylinder();
    draw3DCone();
    renderer.setClearColor( 0xFFFFFF, 1);
    var light = new THREE.PointLight( 0xffffff );
    light.position.z = 40;
    scene.add( light );
    render();
    document.addEventListener("keydown", doKey, false);
}
function render()
{
  renderer.render(scene,camera);
}
function draw3DCylinder()
{
  var cylinderGeometry = new THREE.CylinderGeometry(1,1,4,25,0,false);
```

```
  var material = new THREE.MeshLambertMaterial({
    color: 0x25CA9F,
    shading:THREE.FlatShading,
    overdraw:true
  });

  cylinder = new THREE.Mesh( cylinderGeometry, material);
  cylinder.rotation.set(rotX,rotY,0);
  cylinder.position.set(-3,0,3);
  scene.add(cylinder);
}

function draw3DCone()
{
  //another geometry
  var coneGeometry=new THREE.CylinderGeometry(0,2,4,5,5,false);

  var material = new THREE.MeshLambertMaterial({
                    color:0xFF8000,
                });
  cone = new THREE.Mesh(coneGeometry, material);
  cone.rotation.set(rotX,rotY,0);
        cone.position.set(1, 0, 3);
        scene.add(cone);
}

function doKey(evt) {
    var rotationChanged = true;
    switch (evt.keyCode) {
      case 37: rotY -= 0.04; break;       // left arrow
      case 39: rotY +=  0.04; break;      // right arrow
      case 38: rotX -= 0.04; break;       // up arrow
      case 40: rotX += 0.04; break;       // down arrow
      case 13: rotX = rotY = 0; break;    // return(Enter key)
      case 32: rotX = rotY = 0; break;    //spacebar
      default: rotationChanged = false;
  }
  if (rotationChanged) {
      cylinder.rotation.set(rotX,rotY,0);
      cone.rotation.set(rotX,rotY,0);
      render();
    evt.preventDefault();
  }
}
```

How it works...

This recipe works the same way except that there are two methods named `draw3DCylinder()` and `draw3DCone()` to do the main job. The method used to draw a cylinder or cone is `cylinderGeometry()`. Notice the first parameter (radius) in the method. For a cylinder it is `1` and for a cone it is `0`. Does this ring a bell?

Drawing a 3D sphere and a torus

Some more shapes in 3D are rendered here. The output looks as follows:

3D rotating sphere and doughnut(torus) using three.js

Use arrow keys to make the shapes rotate.
Press Enter key or spacebar to reset

3D rotating sphere and doughnut(torus) using three.js

Use arrow keys to make the shapes rotate.
Press Enter key or spacebar to reset

How to do it...

The HTML code:

```
<html>
<head>
<title>Sphere and torus</title>
<script src="../threeLib/build/three.min.js"></script>
<script src="sphereandring.js">

</script>
</head>
<body onload="init()">
  <center>
  <canvas width="1000" height="600" id="MyCanvasArea"
  style="border:2px solid blue;" tabindex="0">
    Canvas tag is not supported by your browser
  </canvas>
```

```
<h1>3D rotating sphere and doughnut(torus) using three.js</h1>
<h1>Use arrow keys to make the shapes rotate.<br>
Press Enter key or spacebar to reset</h1>
</center>
</body>
</html>
```

The JavaScript code:

```
var can;
var scene;
var camera;
var renderer;
var sphere1,torus1;
var texture;
var rotX=0;
var rotY=0;

function init() {
    can=document.getElementById("MyCanvasArea");

    renderer = new THREE.WebGLRenderer({
      canvas: can
    });


    scene = new THREE.Scene();

    camera = new THREE.PerspectiveCamera(
            35,                     // Field of view(FOV)
            can.width / can.height,      // Aspect ratio
            0.1,                    // Near plane(near)
            10000                   // Far plane(far)
      );

    camera.position.z=10;
    camera.lookAt( scene.position );
    renderer.setClearColor( 0xFFFFFF, 1);

    var light = new THREE.DirectionalLight(); // default white light
    light.position.set(0,0,1);
    scene.add(light);
```

```
      draw3DSphere();
      draw3DTorus();
      render();
      document.addEventListener("keydown", doKey, false);
}
function render()
{
   renderer.render(scene,camera);
}
function draw3DSphere()
{
   var geometry = new THREE.SphereGeometry(1, 50, 50, 0, Math.PI*2,
   0, Math.PI * 2);
   var material = new THREE.MeshBasicMaterial( { map:
   THREE.ImageUtils.loadTexture( 'flowers.jpg' ), overdraw: true } )
   sphere1 = new THREE.Mesh(geometry, material);
   //sphere1.postion.set(1,1,1);
   scene.add(sphere1);
}


function draw3DTorus()
{
   var geometry = new THREE.TorusGeometry(2, 0.5, 25, 100);
   var material = new THREE.MeshBasicMaterial( { map:
   THREE.ImageUtils.loadTexture( 'raj.png' ), overdraw: true } );
   torus1 = new THREE.Mesh(geometry, material);
   scene.add(torus1);
}



function doKey(evt) {
    var rotationChanged = true;
    switch (evt.keyCode) {
      case 37: rotY -= 0.01; break;        // left arrow
      case 39: rotY +=  0.01; break;       // right arrow
      case 38: rotX -= 0.01; break;        // up arrow
      case 40: rotX += 0.01; break;        // down arrow
      case 13: rotX = rotY = 0; break;     // return(Enter key)
      case 32: rotX = rotY = 0; break;     //spacebar
      default: rotationChanged = false;
   }
   if (rotationChanged) {
```

```
        sphere1.rotation.set(rotX,rotY,0);
        torus1.rotation.set(-rotX,-rotY,0);
        render();
    evt.preventDefault();
  }
}
```

How it works...

Here, the methods `SphereGeometry()` and `TorusGeometry()` are used to create the shapes, and the method `MeshBasicMaterial()` is used to create the material the shapes will be made of.

There's more...

Try:

▶   Changing the position of the objects

Drawing 3D text decorated by particles

This recipe focuses on 3D text and particles. The output looks like this:

3D rotating Text using three.js   3D rotating Text using three.js

Use arrow keys to make the text rotate and change the position of particlesUse arrow keys to make the text rotate and change the position of p
Press Enter key or spacebar to reset   Press Enter key or spacebar to reset

How to do it...

The HTML code:

```html
<html>
<body onload="init()">
<script src="../threeLib/build/three.min.js"></script>
<script src="../threeLib/examples/js/geometries/TextGeometry.js"></script>
<script src="../threeLib/examples/js/utils/FontUtils.js"></script>
<script src="../threeLib/examples/fonts/helvetiker_regular.typeface.js"></script>

<script src="text3d.js"></script>

<center>
<canvas width="1000" height="600" id="MyCanvasArea" style="border:2px solid blue;">
    Canvas tag is not supported by your browser
</canvas>
<h1>3D rotating Text using three.js</h1>
<h1>Use arrow keys to make the text rotate and change the position of particles<br>
Press Enter key or spacebar to reset</h1>
</center>
</body>
</html>
```

The JavaScript code:

```javascript
var can;
var scene;
var renderer;
var camera;
var text;
var particleSystem;
var particleGeometry;
var rotX=0;
var rotY=0;
function init()
{
  try
  {
    var can = document.getElementById("MyCanvasArea");
```

```
      renderer = new THREE.WebGLRenderer( { canvas: can, antialias: true
} );
           renderer.setSize(can.width,can.height);

      scene = new THREE.Scene();

           camera = new THREE.PerspectiveCamera
           (50,can.width/can.height, 0.1, 1000);
      camera.position.set(300,10,600);

      var light = new THREE.DirectionalLight(); // default white light
      light.position.set( 0, 0, 1 );
      scene.add(light);

      draw3DText();
      drawParticles();
      render();

      document.addEventListener("keydown", doKey, false);
    }
    catch(e)
    {
      alert(e);
    }
}

function render()
{
  renderer.render(scene,camera);
}

function draw3DText()
{
  var textGeometry= new THREE.TextGeometry("BE  HAPPY");
  var material = new THREE.MeshNormalMaterial();
  text = new THREE.Mesh(textGeometry, material);
      text.rotation.set(rotX,rotY,0);
  scene.add(text);
}
function drawParticles()
{
  particleGeometry=new THREE.Geometry();
  for(var p=0;p<1000;p++)
  {
```

```
        var particle=new THREE.Vector3(Math.random()*500-10, Math.random()
        * 500-200 , Math.random() * 500 - 10);
        particleGeometry.vertices.push(particle);
    }
    var particleMaterial = new THREE.ParticleBasicMaterial({ color:
    0xffa0ee, size: 3 });
    particleSystem = new THREE.ParticleSystem(particleGeometry,
    particleMaterial);
    scene.add(particleSystem);
}
function updateParticles() {

    scene.remove(particleSystem);
    drawParticles();
}
function doKey(evt) {
    var rotationChanged = true;
    switch (evt.keyCode) {
        case 37: rotY -= 0.04; break;         // left arrow
        case 39: rotY +=  0.04; break;        // right arrow
        case 38: rotX -= 0.04; break;         // up arrow
        case 40: rotX += 0.04; break;         // down arrow
        case 13: rotX = rotY = 0; break;      // return(Enter key)
        case 32: rotX = rotY = 0; break;    //spacebar
        default: rotationChanged = false;
    }
    if (rotationChanged) {
        text.rotation.set(rotX,rotY,0);
        updateParticles();
        render();
        evt.preventDefault();
    }
}
```

How it works...

A small change can be seen in the HTML code where the necessary scripts for drawing 3D text are linked. The `TextGeometry` used and the font for the text are the result of using the three JavaScript files `TextGeometry.js`, `FontUtils.js`, and `helvetiker_regular.typeface.js`. There are few fonts supported by three.js.

The methods `draw3DText()` and `drawParticles()` do the job of drawing the text and particles. The same process of creating geometry, applying material to it, and then adding the created geometry to the scene is followed. However, when it comes to the particle system, every particle is pushed into the geometry and then the geometry is rendered.

In this recipe, do observe the method `scene.remove()`, which removes the particles from the scene on every key press (arrow keys) and draws the particles again, so the position of the particle changes. The particle position changes because of the randomization used in drawing the particles, which can be observed in the `drawParticles()` method.

There's more...

Try:

▶ Commenting the `scene.remove()` statement in JavaScript

Drawing a panorama

A panoramic view is always attractive. Here is an output:

3D rotating sphere using three.js   3D rotating sphere using three.js

Use arrow keys to move through the picture.   Use arrow keys to move through the picture.
Press Enter key or spacebar to reset   Press Enter key or spacebar to reset

How to do it...

The HTML code:

```html
<html>
<head>
<title>Panorama</title>
<script src="../threeLib/build/three.min.js"></script>
<script src="panorama.js">
</script>
</head>
<body onload="init()">
  <center>
```

```
    <canvas width="500" height="400" id="MyCanvasArea" style="border:2px
    solid blue;" tabindex="0">
      Canvas tag is not supported by your browser
    </canvas>
    <h1>3D rotating sphere using three.js</h1>
    <h1>Use arrow keys to move through the picture.<br>
    Press Enter key or spacebar to reset</h1>
    </center>
  </body>
  </html>
```

The JavaScript code:

```
var can;
var scene;
var camera;
var renderer;
var sphere1,torus1;
var texture;
var rotX=0;
var rotY=0;

function init() {
    can=document.getElementById("MyCanvasArea");

    renderer = new THREE.WebGLRenderer({
    canvas: can
    });


    scene = new THREE.Scene();

    camera = new THREE.PerspectiveCamera(
            35,                      // Field of view(FOV)
            can.width / can.height,      // Aspect ratio
            0.1,                     // Near plane(near)
            10000                    // Far plane(far)
      );
    camera.position.z=-1;
    camera.lookAt( scene.position );
    renderer.setClearColor( 0xFFFFFF, 1);
```

```
      var light = new THREE.DirectionalLight(); // default white light
      light.position.z=20;
      scene.add(light);


      draw3DSphere();
      render();
      document.addEventListener("keydown", doKey, false);
}
function render()
{
  renderer.render(scene,camera);
}
function draw3DSphere()
{
  var geometry = new THREE.SphereGeometry(1, 50, 50, 0, Math.PI*2,
  0, Math.PI * 2);
  var material = new THREE.MeshBasicMaterial( { map:
  THREE.ImageUtils.loadTexture( 'skyimg.jpg' ), overdraw: true } )
  sphere1 = new THREE.Mesh(geometry, material);
  sphere1.scale.x=-1;
  scene.add(sphere1);
}
function doKey(evt) {
    var rotationChanged = true;
    switch (evt.keyCode) {
      case 37: rotY -= 0.01; break;        // left arrow
      case 39: rotY +=  0.01; break;        // right arrow
      //case 38: rotX -= 0.01; break;        // up arrow
      //case 40: rotX += 0.01; break;        // down arrow
      case 13: rotX = rotY = 0; break;     // return(Enter key)
      case 32: rotX = rotY = 0; break;   //spacebar
      default: rotationChanged = false;
  }
  if (rotationChanged) {
      sphere1.rotation.set(rotX,rotY,0);
      sphere1.scale.x=-1;
      render();
    evt.preventDefault();
  }
}
```

How it works...

The recipe is achieved by a small trick. The camera is inside the 3D object and then rotated on the press of the left and right arrow buttons in the appropriate direction. This is just like standing in a room and watching a single picture being drawn on the walls.

There's more...

Try:

- Using another picture

Drawing a snowman

We have seen independent 3D objects in the previous recipes. Here is an example of a 3D object, a snowman:

Snowman   Snowman

How to do it...

The HTML code:

```
<html>
<head>
<title>Snowman</title>
<script src="../threeLib/build/three.min.js"></script>
<script src="newSnowMan.js">
</script>
</head>
<body onload="init()">
  <center>
```

```
<canvas width="1000" height="600" id="MyCanvasArea"
style="border:2px solid blue;">
  Canvas tag is not supported by your browser
</canvas>
<h1>Snowman</h1>
</center>
</body>
</html>
```

The JavaScript code:

```
var can;
var scene;
var camera;
var renderer;
var snowman;
var particleSystem;
var particleGeometry;
var rotX=0;
var rotY=0;
var clock;

function init() {
    clock=new THREE.Clock();
    can=document.getElementById("MyCanvasArea");

    renderer = new THREE.WebGLRenderer({
    canvas: can,
    antialias: true    //for smooth effect
  });
    scene = new THREE.Scene();

    camera = new THREE.PerspectiveCamera(
            35,                    // Field of view(FOV)
            can.width / can.height,    // Aspect ratio
            0.1,                   // Near plane(near)
            10000                  // Far plane(far)
      );

    camera.position.set(0,0,20);
    camera.lookAt( scene.position );
    drawSnowMan();
    drawParticles();
    renderer.setClearColor( 0x000000, 1);
```

```
      var light = new THREE.PointLight( 0xffffff );
      light.position.z=40;
      scene.add( light );
      render();
}


function drawParticles()
{
  particleGeometry=new THREE.Geometry();
  for(var p=0;p<4000;p++)
  {
    var particle=new THREE.Vector3(Math.random()*2500-100, Math.
    random() * 1500-200 , Math.random() * 1000 - 10);
    particleGeometry.vertices.push(particle);
  }
  var particleMaterial = new THREE.ParticleBasicMaterial({ color:
  0xffffff, size: 3 });
  particleSystem = new THREE.ParticleSystem(particleGeometry,
  particleMaterial);
  scene.add(particleSystem);
}


function render()
{
  requestAnimationFrame(render);
  var delta = clock.getDelta();
  snowman.rotation.y -= delta;
  particleSystem.rotation.y += delta;

  renderer.render(scene,camera);
}
function drawSnowMan()
{
  var meshes=[],geometry,mesh,material;

  var material = new THREE.MeshLambertMaterial( { color: 0xFFFFFF } );
  var woodMaterial = new THREE.MeshLambertMaterial( { color: 0x75691B
} );

  geometry = new THREE.SphereGeometry(1, 50, 50, 0, Math.PI*2, 0,
  Math.PI * 2);
  mesh= new THREE.Mesh(geometry, material);
  meshes.push(mesh);
  mesh.position.y=2;
```

```
geometry = new THREE.SphereGeometry(1.5, 50,50, 0, Math.PI*2, 0,
Math.PI*2);
mesh= new THREE.Mesh(geometry, material);
meshes.push(mesh);
mesh.position.y=0;

geometry = new THREE.SphereGeometry(0.18, 50,50, 0, Math.PI*2, 0,
Math.PI*2);
//var material2 = new THREE.MeshLambertMaterial( { color: 0x000000});
mesh = new THREE.Mesh(geometry, material);
meshes.push(mesh);
mesh.position.set(-0.4,2,1);

geometry = new THREE.SphereGeometry(0.18, 50,50, 0, Math.PI*2, 0,
Math.PI*2);
//material2 = new THREE.MeshLambertMaterial( { color: 0x000000});
mesh = new THREE.Mesh(geometry, material);
meshes.push(mesh);
mesh.position.set(0.4,2,1);

geometry = new THREE.CylinderGeometry(0, 0.3, 2, 50, 50, false) ; //
Cone
var material2 = new THREE.MeshLambertMaterial( { color: 0xFF0000});
mesh1=new THREE.Mesh(geometry,material2);
mesh1.rotation.x=1.8;
mesh1.rotation.y=4;
//mesh1.rotation.z=2;
mesh1.position.set(0,1.6,1);
//scene.add(mesh1);
meshes.push(mesh1);

geometry=mergeMeshes(meshes);
snowman=new THREE.Mesh(geometry, material);
scene.add(snowman);
}
function mergeMeshes (meshes) {
  var combined = new THREE.Geometry();
  for (var i = 0; i < meshes.length; i++) {
    meshes[i].updateMatrix();
    combined.merge(meshes[i].geometry, meshes[i].matrix);
  }
  return combined;
}
```

How it works...

The function `mergeMeshes()` is very important here as it combines all the meshes to form a single 3D object. The merge function (of `THREE.Geometry`) within this function does the job of merging the meshes.

Another important aspect of three.js is used in this recipe, `THREE.Clock`. The clock adds the difference (delta) by which the objects rotate.

There's more...

Try:

▶ Putting a hat on the snowman

8

Game Development

This chapter highlights gaming using a HTML5 Canvas with Phaser. It covers the following topics:

- ▸ Understanding the gaming states
- ▸ Drawing on canvas
- ▸ Playing some music
- ▸ Using sprites from the sprite sheet
- ▸ Demonstrating animation
- ▸ Demonstrating collision
- ▸ Demonstrating physics
- ▸ Game 1 – Fruit Basket
- ▸ Game 2 – Catapult

Introduction

Phaser 2.4.4 is the library I have used for game development. The site `http://phaser.io/` on its home page, under the **Developer Support** link, clearly says *We live and breathe HTML5 games*. Phaser is one of the good choices for HTML5 game development. This chapter is an attempt to inspire readers to develop their own games.

 I enabled WebGL 2.0 prototype in the `chrome://flags`. You need to enable this feature on your browser, so as to execute the given recipes.

Understanding the gaming states

The key to developing a game is to go systematically step by step. Therefore, understanding the basic states of games is necessary. Here, I tried to keep it as simple as possible. The sky is the limit for you to try various experiments using the `Phaser` library with the HTML5 Canvas. In this recipe, you will see an updated date and time. The purpose of this recipe is to let you understand the states of a game. The output shown here is of less importance than the code:

```
Fri Jan 22 2016 05:27:13 GMT+0530 (India Standard Time)
```

How to do it...

The recipe is as follows:

```html
<html>
  <head>
    <meta charset="UTF-8" />
  <title>The Gaming States</title>
    <script src="../phaser-master/build/phaser.min.js"></script>
  </head>
  <body>
    <script type="text/javascript">
      var game = new Phaser.Game(800, 600, Phaser.CANVAS, 'phaser-
      example', { preload: preload, create: create,update:
      update,render: render});
      var today;
      function preload()
      {
        //here we load any resources required
        //like images, audios etc..
      }
      function create()
      {
        //here we create objects and variables to be used
      }
      function update()
      {
```

```
        today=new Date();
      }
      function render()
      {
        game.debug.text(today,100,100);
      }
    </script>
  </body>
</html>
```

How it works...

A very important statement in this recipe is as follows:

```
var game = new Phaser.Game(800, 600, Phaser.CANVAS, 'phaser-example',
{ preload: preload, create: create,update: update,render: render});
```

This shows the usage of canvas in Phaser. You might have noticed that `Phaser.CANVAS` is the property, which indicates the usage of Canvas. There are two more options: `Phaser.WEBGL` and `Phaser.AUTO`. The functions listed in the constructor can be understood as states. They are preload, create, update, and render. The fifth parameter in the constructor is an array of a state-function pair. It is not mandatory to have all the functions. In this recipe, the `preload()` and `create()` functions have no operation to do. However, the `update()` and `render()` functions are periodically called.

Drawing on canvas

Drawing on canvas is possible through `phaser.js` using the same functions and properties as we used in core JavaScript. Here is an output:

How to do it...

The HTML code is as follows:

```html
<html>
  <head>
    <meta charset="UTF-8" />
  <title>The Canvas Drawing</title>
    <script src="../phaser-master/build/phaser.min.js"></script>
  </head>
  <body>
    <script type="text/javascript">
      var game = new Phaser.Game(800, 600, Phaser.CANVAS, 'phaser-
      example', { render: render});

      function render()
      {
        game.context.fillStyle = 'rgb(255,0,0)';
        game.context.beginPath();
        game.context.linewidth=10;
        game.context.fillRect(game.width/2-10,game.
        height/2-50,100,100);
        game.context.fillRect(game.width/2-40,game.
        height/2-150,100,100);
        game.context.fillRect(game.width/2-100,game.height/2,100,100);
        game.context.closePath();
      }
    </script>
  </body>
</html>
```

How it works...

In the prior chapters on canvas, we were using statements such as `ctx.fillRect(...)` to draw a rectangle, where `ctx` was the context. Here, the `game.context.fillRect(...)` statement is used to draw the rectangle. The API is similar to the canvas API. The game wraps the context of the canvas on which we draw.

There's more...

Try drawing something different, may be a smiley.

Playing some music

One of the lively aspects of games is the music. Here is a crisp recipe to play music. The output of this recipe looks as follows. Of course, unless you try this example, you will not be able to listen to the music:

How to do it...

The HTML code is as follows:

```
<html>
  <head>
    <meta charset="UTF-8" />
  <title>Playing Music</title>
    <script src="../phaser-master/build/phaser.min.js"></script>
  </head>
  <body>
    <script type="text/javascript">
      var game = new Phaser.Game(800, 600, Phaser.CANVAS, 'phaser-
      example', {preload: preload,create: create,update: update,
      render: render});
      var music;
      var play;
      var stop;
      function preload()
      {
```

```
      game.load.audio('bkgmusic',['music/background1.mp3']);
      game.load.image('play','gameimages/playbutton.png');
      game.load.image('stop','gameimages/stopbutton.png');
    }
    function create()
    {
      music = game.add.audio('bkgmusic');
      var play=game.add.sprite(100,100,'play');
      var stop=game.add.sprite(300,100,'stop');

      play.inputEnabled=true;
      play.events.onInputDown.add(playmusic,this);

      stop.inputEnabled=true;
      stop.events.onInputDown.add(stopmusic,this);

      music.volume=0.3;
      music.loop=true;
      music.play();

    }

    function stopmusic()
    {
      if(music.isPlaying)
        music.stop();
    }
    function playmusic()
    {
      if(!music.isPlaying)
        music.play();
    }
    function update(){}
    function render()
    {
      game.debug.
      game.debug.soundInfo(music, 200, 200);
    }
  </script>
 </body>
</html>
```

How it works...

This recipe is a very simple recipe to just play and stop the music with a button (actually an image) click. So here, the click event is handled by the following statements:

```
play.events.onInputDown.add(playmusic,this);&
stop.events.onInputDown.add(stopmusic,this);
```

Then the `playmusic` and `stopmusic` methods do the needful. In this recipe, music is an object that is made by loading the music file. This objects status is changed as per the requirement. Here, we use `music.play()` and `music.stop()`. Can you try pausing and resuming?

There's more...

Try the following:

- Change the music. You may want to play their own.
- Add a pause button and make it work.

Using sprites from the sprite sheet

This recipe shows you fruit falling from top of the screen and slowly filling the canvas. It shows the usage of a sprite sheet and creation of sprites. The output looks as shown here:

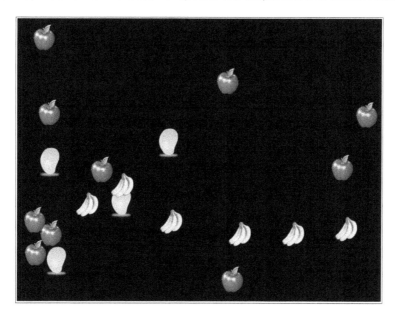

How to do it...

The HTML code is as follows:

```
<html>
  <head>
    <meta charset="UTF-8" />
    <title>Sprites</title>
    <script src="../phaser-master/build/phaser.min.js"></script>
  </head>
  <body>
    <script type="text/javascript">
      var game = new Phaser.Game(800, 600, Phaser.CANVAS, 'phaser-
      example', {preload: preload,create: create});
      var group1;
      var sprite;
      var timer;
      function preload() {
      game.load.spritesheet('fandi', 'gameimages/fruitsinsects.png',
      64, 64);
      }
      function create() {
        game.physics.startSystem(Phaser.Physics.ARCADE);
        group1=game.add.group();
        group1.enableBody=true;
        timer=game.time.create(false);
        timer.loop(1000,releaseObject,this);
        timer.start();
      }

      function releaseObject()
      {
      var rnum=game.rnd.between(0,2);                    sprite=group1.
      create(game.rnd.between(1,game.width),0,'fandi',rnum);
          sprite.body.collideWorldBounds=true;
          sprite.body.gravity.x=game.rnd.integerInRange(-50,50);
          sprite.body.gravity.y=100+Math.random()*100;
          sprite.body.bounce.setTo(0.9,0.9);
      }

    </script>
  </body>
</html>
```

How it works...

A sprite sheet is a series of images that can be used in animation. Here the sprite sheet we use has different images. The sprite sheet has three fruits and three insects:

However, when you execute the recipe, only the first three fruits fall down. This is because of these two statements:

```
var rnum=game.rnd.between(0,2);

sprite=group1.create(game.rnd.between(1,game.width),0,'fandi',rnum);
```

Here, `rnum` is a random number between 0 and 2. You can imagine the sprite sheet as an array of frames. The sprite is created from the first three images, which is `apple` with frame number 0, `banana` with frame number 1, or `mango` with frame number 2. They are created with the x coordinate being anything between 1 and `game.width` and the y coordinate being 0.

There's more...

Try the following:

- Let only insects fall
- Change the scale of the sprite
- Create your own sprite sheet and use it

Demonstrating animation

Animation adds life and spice in a game. Here, rather than the effect, the recipe focuses on the API usage. The recipe is simple and can be used to implement an educational concept (flash card). The output of the recipe is as follows:

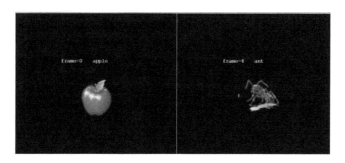

How to do it...

The HTML code is as follows:

```
<html>
  <head>
    <meta charset="UTF-8" />
  <title>Animation Example</title>
    <script src="../phaser-master/build/phaser.min.js"></script>
  </head>
  <body>
    <script type="text/javascript">
      var game = new Phaser.Game(800, 600, Phaser.CANVAS, 'phaser-
      example', {preload: preload,create: create,render: render});
      var image;
      var imagename='';
      function preload() {
        game.load.spritesheet('image', 'gameimages/fruitsinsects.png',
        64, 64,6);
      }
      function create() {
        image= game.add.sprite(300, 200, 'image');
        image.scale.setTo(2,2);
        var flash=image.animations.add('flash');
        image.animations.play('flash', 0.5, false);
      }
      function render()
      {
        game.debug.text('frame='+image.frame,250,150);
        switch(image.frame)
        {
          case 0:
            imagename='apple';
            break;
          case 1:
            imagename='banana';
            break;
          case 2:
            imagename='mango';
            break;
          case 3:
            imagename='a bug';
            break;
```

```
      case 4:
        imagename='ant';
        break;
      case 5:
        imagename='spider';
        break;
    }
    game.debug.text(imagename,350,150);
  }
</script>
</body>
</html>
```

How it works...

As mentioned before, a sprite sheet is a series of images, and every image is technically understood as a frame. We can understand a sprite sheet as a collection of frames. In the output, purposely the frame number has been displayed so that the user understands that the images displayed are a part of a sprite sheet and not an individual image. Here, the same sprite sheet is used as in the previous example. Unlike the previous example, here all the frames are used.

There's more...

Try the following:

- ▸ Use another sprite sheet.
- ▸ Increase or reduce the speed of the display.
- ▸ Put the animation in a loop.

Demonstrating collision

Collision is one of the important aspects of gaming. Here, in this recipe, a car bangs with a bird and there is an explosion. The output looks as follows:

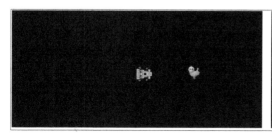 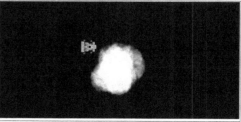

How to do it...

The HTML code is as follows:

```html
<html>
  <head>
    <meta charset="UTF-8" />
  <title>Collision</title>
    <script src="../phaser-master/build/phaser.min.js"></script>
  </head>
  <body>
    <script type="text/javascript">
      var game = new Phaser.Game(800, 600, Phaser.CANVAS, 'phaser-
      example', {preload: preload,create: create,update: update});
      var car1;
      var car2;

      function preload() {
        game.load.image('car1','gameimages/car1.png');
        game.load.image('bird','gameimages/bluebird.png');
        game.load.spritesheet('explosion','gameimages/explosion.png',
        64,64,23);
      }

      function create() {

        game.physics.startSystem(Phaser.Physics.ARCADE);

        car1=game.add.sprite(100,100,'car1');
        car1.enableBody=true;

        bird=game.add.sprite(500,100,'bird');
        bird.enableBody=true;
        bird.scale.setTo(0.1,0.1);

        game.physics.arcade.enable(car1);
        game.physics.arcade.enable(bird);

      }
      function update()
      {
        game.physics.arcade.collide(car1, bird, explode, null, this);
        car1.body.velocity.x=200;
      }
```

```
function explode(car1,bird)
{
  var image= game.add.sprite(bird.body.x,bird.body.y-10,
  'explosion');
  image.animations.killOnComplete=true;
  image.scale.setTo(2,2);
  var boom=image.animations.add('boom');
  image.animations.play('boom', 20, false,true);
  bird.kill();
  bird.destroy();
}
</script>
</body>
</html>
```

How it works...

This recipe is all about two sprites and their collision, which results in an explosion.
This is shown by incorporating animation. The two sprites are a car and a bird (thanks to
http://phaser.io/ for the well-created images). When the car hits the bird, an event
collide happens, and it is handled by the function explode() where the animation is
played and then killed after it completes one loop.

There's more...

Try the following:

▶   Kill the car.

▶   Use another effect instead of explosion. Remember, you need to have a sprite sheet.

Demonstrating physics

Actually, we have already witnessed physics in the previous recipes as they contained velocity and gravity. In this recipe, it is vector calculus which is demonstrated. The output of this recipe looks as follows:

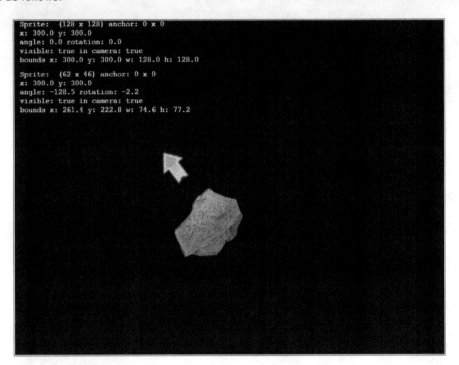

How to do it...

The HTML code is as follows:

```
<html>
  <head>
    <meta charset="UTF-8" />
  <title>Physics</title>
    <script src="../phaser-master/build/phaser.min.js"></script>
  </head>
  <body>
    <script type="text/javascript">
      var game = new Phaser.Game(800, 600, Phaser.CANVAS, 'phaser-
      example', { preload: preload, create: create,update: update,
      render: render});
      var stone;
```

```
      function preload()
      {
        game.load.image('stone','gameimages/stone.png');
        game.load.image('arrow', 'gameimages/arrow.png');
      }
      function create()
      {
        game.physics.startSystem(Phaser.Physics.ARCADE);
        game.physics.arcade.checkCollision.left=true;
        stone=game.add.sprite(300,300,'stone');
        stone.enableBody=true;
        game.physics.enable(stone, Phaser.Physics.ARCADE);
        stone.inputEnabled=true;
        stone.input.enableDrag(true);
        stone.body.allowRotation=true;
        stone.outOfBoundsKills=true;
        arrow=game.add.sprite(300,300,'arrow');
        stone.events.onDragStop.add(hit,this);
      }
      function hit()
      {
        stone.rotation=Math.atan2(stone.body.velocity.y,stone.body.
        velocity.x);

        if(arrow.angle>=0)
          stone.angle=arrow.angle-180;
        else
          stone.angle=arrow.angle+180;

        stone.body.velocity.x=Math.cos(stone.rotation)*100;
        stone.body.velocity.y=Math.sin(stone.rotation)*100;
      }
      function update()
      {
        arrow.rotation=game.physics.arcade.angleToPointer(arrow);
      }
      function render()
      {
        game.debug.spriteInfo(stone,10,10);
        game.debug.spriteInfo(arrow,10,100);
      }
    </script>
  </body>
</html>
```

How it works...

The code is all about dragging a stone and releasing it so that it accelerates in the opposite direction of the pull. This is like a boy using a catapult to hit a stone to some distant object. The data shown in the recipe appears, as we are able to show this sprite information through the render function, which gets called periodically.

The `hit()` function is called as soon as the dragging of stone stops. You can see this in the following statement:

```
stone.events.onDragStop.add(hit,this);
```

The `hit()` method is the place where the physics and vector calculus is implemented. The calculations are done with respect to the green-colored arrow image. The angle of the stone is made opposite to the angle of the arrow. Then, the appropriate velocity is applied to the stone. You can observe this in the snippet given here:

```
stone.rotation=Math.atan2(stone.body.velocity.y,stone.body.
velocity.x);

if(arrow.angle>=0)
    stone.angle=arrow.angle-180;
else
    stone.angle=arrow.angle+180;

stone.body.velocity.x=Math.cos(stone.rotation)*100;
stone.body.velocity.y=Math.sin(stone.rotation)*100;
```

There's more...

Try the following:

▸ Scale down the image

Game 1 – Fruit Basket

This is a very simple game, which is about collecting the fruits and not the insects. For every fruit gathered, you get 10 points, and for every insect, you get -15 points. The output is as follows:

How to do it...

The HTML code is as follows:

```html
<html>
  <head>
    <meta charset="UTF-8" />
  <title>Game1: Fruit Basket</title>
    <script src="../phaser-master/build/phaser.min.js"></script>
  </head>
  <body>
    <h1>Fruit Basket</h1>
    <h2>Use arrow keys to move left or right</h2>
    <h2>Press ESC whenever you want to stop the game</h2>
    <script type="text/javascript">
    var game = new Phaser.Game(800, 600, Phaser.AUTO, 'phaser-
    example', { preload: preload, create: create,update: update});
      var group1;
      var basket;
      var timer;
      var cursors;
      var sprite;
      var score=0;
      var scoreText;
```

```
var esckey;
var gameOverText;
function preload()
{
  game.load.image('basket', 'gameimages/basket3.png');
  game.load.spritesheet('fandi', 'gameimages/fruitsinsects.png',
  64, 64);
  game.load.image('sky','gameimages/starrysky.png');
}
function create()
{
  game.physics.startSystem(Phaser.Physics.ARCADE);
  game.physics.arcade.checkCollision.down=false;

  background=game.add.image(0,0,'sky');

  cursors = game.input.keyboard.createCursorKeys();

  spacekey=game.input.keyboard.addKey(Phaser.Keyboard.UP);
  esckey=game.input.keyboard.addKey(Phaser.Keyboard.ESC);

  basket=game.add.sprite(game.width/2,game.height-50,'basket');
  basket.scale.setTo(2,2);
  game.physics.arcade.enable(basket);

  basket.body.collideWorldBounds=true;
  basket.body.immovable=true;
  basket.body.allowGravity=false;

  group1=game.add.group();
  group1.enableBody=true;
  group1.physicsBodyType=Phaser.Physics.ARCADE;

  timer=game.time.create(false);
  timer.loop(2000,releaseObject,this);
  timer.start();

  scoreText = game.add.text(10, 10, 'Your score: 0', { font:
  "20px Arial", fill: "#000000", align: "left" });
}

function update()
{
```

```
game.physics.arcade.collide(basket,group1,collisionHandler,
null,this);
if(cursors.left.isDown)
{
  basket.body.velocity.x-=20;
}
else if(cursors.right.isDown)
{
  basket.body.velocity.x+=20;
}
if(esckey.isDown)
{
  reset();
  gameOverText=game.add.text(game.width/2-50, game.height/2,
  'Your Score is'+score + '\nThank you for playing
  FruitBasket', { font: "20px Arial", fill: "#000000", align:
  "left" });
}
}
function collisionHandler(basket,sprite)
{
  if(sprite.frame<3)
    score=score+10;
  else
    score=score-15;
  scoreText.text='Your score: '+score;
  sprite.kill();
  sprite.destroy();
}
function releaseObject()
{
  var rnum=game.rnd.between(0,5);
  sprite=group1.create(game.rnd.between(1,game.width),0,'fandi',
  rnum);
  sprite.body.collideWorldBounds=true;
  sprite.body.gravity.x=game.rnd.integerInRange(-50,50);
  sprite.body.gravity.y=100+Math.random()*100;
  sprite.body.bounce.setTo(0.9,0.9);

}
</script>
</body>
</html>
```

How it works...

There are many functions, which work together to achieve the output. The chronology of activities in this game is given here:

1. Load the required images.

2. Create the objects with their properties set as per requirement, and then begin with the initial display. The timer here is set for 2 seconds.

3. Every 2 seconds, an object falls from the top from a random position.

4. The update function takes care of the movement of the basket. Also, the collide event is handled here by calling the `collisionHandler()` method. The *Esc* key is also handled here for stopping the game.

5. What to do when the fruit/insect collides with the basket is decided in the `collisionHandler()`, where the score is updated and the objects that hit the basket are killed.

There's more...

Try the following:

▶ Make the objects fall with a random speed

Game 2 – Catapult

Though the name is Catapult, you will not see a catapult while playing the game. However, with some work on graphics, you can surely add a catapult. I named it as Catapult as it has the functionality of catapult (drag and release). In the game, you have to drag and release the stone to make it hit the objects. The output looks like the following:

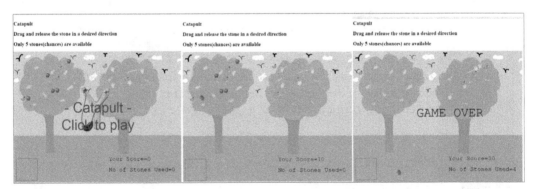

How to do it...

The HTML code is as follows:

```html
<html>
  <head>
    <meta charset="UTF-8" />
  <title>Catapult</title>
    <script src="../phaser-master/build/phaser.min.js"></script>
  </head>
  <body>
    <h2>Catapult</h2>
    <h2>Drag and release the stone in a desired direction</h2>
    <h2>Only 5 stones(chances) are available</h2>
    <script type="text/javascript">
      var game = new Phaser.Game(800, 600, Phaser.AUTO, 'phaser-
      example', { preload: preload, create: create,update: update,
      render: render});
      var stone;
      var backgr;
      var music;
      var catchFlag = false;
      var speed=100;
      var image;
      var text;
      var score;
      var sprite;
      var fruits;
      var birds;
      var bird;
      var points={x:10,y:game.height};
      var box={width:100,height:100};
      var isScoreUpdated;
      var score;
      var stoneCount;
      var maxCount;
      function preload()
      {
        game.load.image('backgr','gameimages/back1.png');
        game.load.image('frontimage','gameimages/catapult.png');
        game.load.spritesheet('fruits','gameimages/fruitsinsects.png',
        64, 64);
        game.load.image('arrow', 'gameimages/arrow.png');
        game.load.image('bird','gameimages/orangebird.png');
```

```
            game.load.image('stone','gameimages/stone.png');
            game.load.audio('bkgmusic',['music/background1.mp3']);
        }
        function create()
        {
          isScoreUpdated=0;
          score=0;
          stoneCount=0;
          maxCount=5;
          game.physics.startSystem(Phaser.Physics.ARCADE);
          game.physics.arcade.checkCollision.left=true;
          cursors = game.input.keyboard.createCursorKeys();

          backgr=game.add.sprite(game.world.centerX-game.world.centerX,
          game.world.centerY-game.world.centerY,'backgr');
          image=game.add.sprite(game.world.centerX-100,game.world.
          centerY-200, 'frontimage');
          image.scale.setTo(0.5,0.5);

          text = game.add.text(game.world.centerX, game.world.centerY,
          "- Catapult -\nClick to play", { font: "65px Arial", fill:
          "#0000ff", align: "center" });

          text.anchor.setTo(0.5, 0.5);

          game.input.onDown.addOnce(removeAlpha, this);

          arrow = game.add.sprite(points.x+40,points.y-75, 'arrow');

          game.physics.enable(arrow, Phaser.Physics.ARCADE);

          arrow.anchor.setTo(1, 1);
          arrow.body.moves = false;
          arrow.body.allowGravity = false;
          arrow.alpha = 0;
          arrow.body.allowRotation=false;

          createFruits();
          createBirds();

          createStone();

          stone.alpha=0;
```

```
  music = game.add.audio('bkgmusic');
  music.volume=0.3;
  music.loop=true;
  music.play();
}
function update()
{
  game.physics.arcade.collide(stone, fruits,
  fruitCollisionHandler, null, this);
  game.physics.arcade.collide(stone, birds,
  birdCollisionHandler, null, this);
  if(stone.body.onFloor())
  {
    stone.kill();
    stone.destroy();
    createStone();
    stoneCount=stoneCount+1;
  }
  if(stoneCount==maxCount)
  {
    stone.kill();
    stone.destroy();
    game.debug.text('GAME OVER',game.width/2-100,game.height/2,
    '#0000bf','58px courier');
  }

  isScoreUpdated=0;
}
function fruitCollisionHandler(stone,sprite)
{
  sprite.body.gravity.y=700;
  stone.body.gravity.y=400;
  if(isScoreUpdated==0)
  {
    score=score+10;
    isScoreUpdated=1;
  }
  sprite.kill();
  sprite.destroy();
}
function birdCollisionHandler(stone,bird)
{
  bird.body.gravity.y=300;
  stone.body.gravity.y=200;
```

```
          score=score-15;
        bird.kill();
        bird.destroy();
      }
    function render()
    {
      game.context.strokeStyle = 'rgb(255,0,0)';
      game.context.beginPath();
      game.context.linewidth=4;
      game.context.rect(points.x,points.y-110,100,100);
      game.context.stroke();
      game.context.closePath();
      game.debug.text('Your Score=' + score,450,500,'#ff0000',
      '28px courier');
      game.debug.text('No of Stones Used=' + stoneCount,450,550,
      '#0000f0','28px courier');
      if(stoneCount==5)
        game.debug.text('GAME OVER',game.width/2-100,game.height/2,
        '#0000bf','58px courier');

    }
    function removeAlpha()
    {
      stone.alpha=1;
      fruits.alpha=1;
      birds.alpha=1;
      image.kill();
      text.destroy();
    }
    function createFruits()
    {
      fruits=game.add.group();
      fruits.enableBody=true;
      fruits.physicsBodyType=Phaser.Physics.ARCADE;

      for (var i = 0; i< 5; i++)
      {
      sprite=fruits.create(game.rnd.integerInRange(40,260), game.
      rnd.integerInRange(20,210), 'fruits',0);
        sprite.body.collideWorldBounds=true;
        sprite.scale.setTo(0.4,0.4);
      }
      for (var i = 0; i< 5; i++)
      {
```

```
    sprite=fruits.create(game.rnd.integerInRange(440,650), game.
    rnd.integerInRange(40,210), 'fruits',2);
      sprite.body.collideWorldBounds=true;
      sprite.scale.setTo(0.4,0.4);
    }
    fruits.alpha=1;
}
function createBirds()
{
  birds=game.add.group();
  birds.enableBody=true;
  birds.physicsBodyType=Phaser.Physics.ARCADE;

  for (var i = 0; i< 3; i++)
  {
  bird=birds.create(game.rnd.integerInRange(20,260), game.rnd.
  integerInRange(25,210), 'bird');
    bird.body.collideWorldBounds=true;
    bird.scale.setTo(0.4,0.4);
  }
  for (var i = 0; i< 3; i++)
  {
  bird=birds.create(game.rnd.integerInRange(400,650), game.rnd.
  integerInRange(25,210), 'bird');
    bird.body.collideWorldBounds=true;
    bird.scale.setTo(0.4,0.4);
  }
  birds.alpha=1;
}
function createStone()
{
  stone=game.add.sprite(points.x+40,points.y-75,'stone');
  game.physics.enable(stone, Phaser.Physics.ARCADE);
  stone.enableBody=true;
  stone.body.collideWorldBounds=true;
  stone.scale.setTo(0.2,0.2);
  stone.body.bounce.set(0.5);
  stone.inputEnabled=true;
  stone.input.enableDrag(true);
  stone.events.onDragStop.add(hit,this);
}
function gameOver()
```

```
        {
            game.debug.text('No of Stones Used=' + stoneCount,450,550,
            '#0000f0','28px courier');
        }
        function hit()
        {
            stone.body.gravity.y=10;
            stone.rotation=Math.atan2(stone.body.velocity.y,stone.body.
            velocity.x);
            arrow.rotation=game.physics.arcade.angleToPointer(arrow);
            if(arrow.angle>=0)
                stone.angle=arrow.angle-180;
            else
                stone.angle=arrow.angle+180;

            stone.body.velocity.x=Math.cos(stone.rotation)*250;
            stone.body.velocity.y=Math.sin(stone.rotation)*250;
        }
    </script>

    </body>
</html>
```

How it works...

The game Catapult is about dropping fruits with a stone. The game contains loads of functions. However, all aspects of the game are covered in the prior recipes. The game exhibits few physics principles and canvas drawing.

There's more...

Try the following:

- Change the speed of the stone depending on the dragging
- Increase the number of chances to hit

9

Interoperability and Deployment

This chapter highlights the interoperability, compatibility, and deployment of applications/games with respect to different browsers and devices. The topics covered are as follows:

- ▶ Understanding interoperability
- ▶ Styling text and background using CSS
- ▶ Deploying a game on Android mobile

Introduction

Browser and device compatibility is an important issue when it comes to the execution of programs. Also, the deployment of applications and games on compatible devices is another concern. This chapter gives an overview of browser compatibility with respect to HTML5 Canvas and **CSS** (**Cascaded Style Sheet**). It also covers a game recipe, which can be deployed on mobiles.

CSS is a language that helps HTML/XML to present a document with style. Thus, the role of CSS is to apply styles. Throughout the chapters, I had focused on HTML5 Canvas and JavaScript. This chapter, however, introduces CSS through some crisp recipes. I will be using only external CSS. I believe that you already know the other two types (internal and inline).

Understanding interoperability

HTML5 Canvas is supported on almost all browsers. However, browsers with older versions do not support it, for example, IE 8. But for IE 9 onwards, support is available for canvas. There are many other browsers such as Chrome, Safari, Opera, Android browsers, and so on, that support HTML5 Canvas.

WebGL rendering is supported by Firefox and Chrome. However, few versions of other browsers do support WebGL rendering.

`Phaser.js` is a library that supports HTML5 Canvas and WebGL and can be used on all browsers, which can understand HTML5 Canvas.

Browser interoperability and device interoperability is very important. The games or applications developed in HTML5 Canvas can work on most devices that can support compatible browsers. The WebGL part is dependent on the hardware of the device.

Styling text and background using CSS

As mentioned earlier, CSS can be used for styling and here is a simple demo of styling text. The output of the recipe is given here:

How to do it

The recipe is as follows:

The HTML code:

```
<html>
<head>
  <title>CSS Background Example</title>
  <link rel="stylesheet" type="text/css" href="stylesheet.css">
</head>
<body class="main">
  <center>
  <table border=1>
    <tr class="firstrow">
      <td height="200" width="800">
        <h1 id="title">CSS Demo</h1>
      </td>
    </tr>
    <tr class="secondrow">
      <td height="400" width="800" align="center">
        <p>This is a simple demo of CSS exhibiting usage of a tag-
        specific style and selectors.<br>
          The file background.css contains all the styling properties
          which are applied here on the HTML Page.
        </p>
      </td>
    </tr>
  </table>
  </center>
</body>
</html>
```

The CSS code:

```
.main {
background: linear-gradient(blue, white,pink,#00AA88);
}
p {
font-family: "Lucida Console";
font-size: 30px;
color:#EFAA98;
letter-spacing: 2px;
text-align:center;
text-shadow: 3px3px4px black;
```

```
}
.firstrow
{
    background: radial-gradient(circle,black,white);
}
.secondrow
{
    background: url("Background.png");
}
#title
{
color: orange;
text-align: center;
font-family: "Comic Sans MS";
font-size: 60px;
text-shadow: 2px2px3px white,
    4px4px5px green;
}
```

How it works...

Here, the CSS code is very important and the trick to styling the page lies in this code. There is a lot to explore in CSS. The `.main` mentioned in the code happens to be a class and is used as a value for the class property of the element, as you may see it in the `<body>` element of HTML code. Similarly, `.firstRow` and `.secondRow` are classes. `#title` happens to be an ID, which is used for styling the `h1` tag. Also, CSS shows you the usage of normal element styling through the `<p>` tag. Observe the properties mentioned for styling paragraph elements shown in the `.css` file.

There's more...

Try using your own styles. You can do this easily if you know the correct properties of various HTML5 elements.

Deploying a game on Android mobile

The deployment of a game on a mobile phone is quite interesting. First, let me tell you that all the experiments for the recipe were performed on an Android phone. The output of the game would be the same as seen in the previous chapter for the game named Fruit Basket. However, as the window of every device is different, the size of the game will change as per the display screen.

How to do it

The recipe is as follows:

The HTML code:

```html
<html>
  <head>
    <meta charset="UTF-8" />
    <title>Game1: Fruit Basket</title>
      <scriptsrc="js/phaser.min.js"></script>

      <link rel="stylesheet" type="text/css" href="css/stylesheet1.css"/>
  </head>
  <body>
    <center>
    <div id="header" align="center">
      <h1 id="title">Fruit Basket</h1>
      <p>Touch on left or right of the basket to move it.<br>
      Double tap whenever you get bored</p>
    </div>
    <script type="text/javascript">
      var wiw=window.outerWidth;
      var wih=window.outerHeight;
      var gratio=wiw/wih;
      var game = new Phaser.Game(Math.ceil(wiw*gratio),Math.ceil
      (wih*gratio), Phaser.CANVAS, 'phaser-example', {boot:boot,
      preload: preload, create: create,update: update});
      var group1;
      var basket;
      var timer;
      var cursors;
      var sprite;
      var score=0;
      var scoreText;
      var esckey;
      var gameOverText;
      var imageX;
      var imageY;
      var gameStatus="started";
      function boot()
      {
        this.scale.scaleMode=Phaser.ScaleManager.USER_SCALE;
        this.scale.pageAlignHorizontally = true;
```

```
      this.scale.pageAlignVertically = true;
      this.scale.forceOrientation(false,true);
      this.scale.refresh();
  }
  function preload()
  {
    game.load.image('basket', 'images/basket3.png');
    game.load.spritesheet('fandi', 'images/fruitsinsects.png', 64,
    64);
  }
  function create()
  {
    game.physics.startSystem(Phaser.Physics.ARCADE);
    game.physics.arcade.checkCollision.down=false;

    game.stage.backgroundColor='#ABCDEF';

    cursors = game.input.keyboard.createCursorKeys();

    spacekey=game.input.keyboard.addKey(Phaser.Keyboard.UP);
    esckey=game.input.keyboard.addKey(Phaser.Keyboard.ESC);

    basket=game.add.sprite(game.width/2,game.height-30,'basket');
    basket.scale.setTo(1,1);
    game.physics.arcade.enable(basket);

    basket.body.collideWorldBounds=true;
    basket.body.immovable=true;
    basket.body.allowGravity=false;

    group1=game.add.group();
    group1.enableBody=true;
    group1.physicsBodyType=Phaser.Physics.ARCADE;

    timer=game.time.create(false);
    timer.loop(2000,releaseObject,this);
    timer.start();

    scoreText = game.add.text(10, 10, 'Your score: 0', { font:
    "20px Arial", fill: "#000000", align: "left" });
    game.input.onTap.add(onTap,this);
  }
```

```
function onTap(pointer,doubleTap)
{
  if(doubleTap)
  {
    if(gameStatus=="started")
    {
      timer.stop();
      sprite.kill();
      sprite.destroy();
      gameStatus="gameover";
      gameOverText=game.add.text(game.width/2, game.height/2,
      'Score\n'+score + '\nDouble Tap \nto restart', { font:
      "20px Arial", fill: "#000000", align: "left" });
      score=0;
    }
    else
    {
      game.world.remove(gameOverText);
      gameStatus="started";
      timer.start();
      game.state.restart();
    }
  }
  else
  {
    imageX=basket.body.x;
    imageY=basket.body.y;
    if(game.input.activePointer.y>=imageY-100 &&game.input.
    activePointer.y<=imageY+basket.body.height+50 )
    {
      if(game.input.activePointer.x<imageX)
      {
        //move left
        basket.body.velocity.x-=200;
      }
      else if(game.input.activePointer.x>imageX)
      {
        //move right
        basket.body.velocity.x+=200;
      }
    }
  }
}
function update()
```

```
            {
              game.physics.arcade.collide(basket,group1,collisionHandler,
              null,this);

            }
          function collisionHandler(basket,sprite)
            {
              if(sprite.frame<3)
                score=score+10;
              else
                score=score-15;
                scoreText.text='Your score: '+score;
                sprite.kill();
                sprite.destroy();
            }
          function releaseObject()
            {
              var rnum=game.rnd.between(0,5);
              sprite=group1.create(game.rnd.between(1,game.width),0,'fandi',
              rnum);
              sprite.body.collideWorldBounds=true;
              sprite.body.gravity.x=game.rnd.integerInRange(-50,50);
              sprite.body.gravity.y=100+Math.random()*100;
              sprite.body.bounce.setTo(0.9,0.9);
              sprite.scale.setTo(0.5,0.5);
            }
        </script>
        </center>
      </body>
    </html>
```

The CSS code:

```
body{
   background-image: url("../images/starrysky.png");
   background-repeat: repeat;
}
p {
font-family: "Lucida Console";
font-size: 90%;
font-bold: true;
color:#FF7A98;
letter-spacing: 2px;
text-align:center;
text-shadow: 3px3px4px black;
```

```
}
#title
{
color: orange;
text-align: center;
font-family: "Comic Sans MS";
font-size: 130%;
text-shadow: 2px2px3px white,
    4px4px5px green;
}
```

How it works...

The change in the recipe compared to the recipe mentioned in the previous chapter is as follows:

```
var wiw=window.outerWidth;
    var wih=window.outerHeight;
    var gratio=wiw/wih;
    var game = new Phaser.Game(Math.ceil(wiw*gratio),Math.ceil
    (wih*gratio), Phaser.CANVAS, 'phaser-example', {boot:boot,preload:
    preload, create: create,update: update});
```

We get the width and height of the window of the device. Then, we calculate the ratio by dividing width by height and use it to draw the game dimensions. Later, scaling is required, so the objects are scaled as per the game size. The code for scaling is written once and is included in the `boot()` function. Another change you can see is the inclusion of CSS to beautify the game a bit. Check out the background and the rendered text for the game. This can be seen in the first few lines of code.

Another important change in the code is about handling the touch events. This is done through the method `onTap` which handles a single as well as double tap through the branching statements.

Note that the APK file is created by uploading files to the GitHub repository, and then building through PhoneGap. The explanation for this is out of scope of this book.

There's more...

Try deploying the other game on your mobile.

Index

Symbols

3D cubes
  drawing 174-178
3D cylinder
  drawing 179-182
3D objects
  rendering 170-173
3D sphere
  drawing 182-185
3D text
  drawing, with decorated particles 185-189
  drawing, with shadows 29-32

A

acceleration
  demonstrating 68, 69
  working 70, 71
addColorStop() method 48
Android mobile
  game, deploying on 226-231
animated clipping
  about 112
  working 115
animate() function 75
animation
  combining, with events 142-145
  demonstrating 205-207
animation class
  creating 68
arc1
  drawing 12-15
arc2
  drawing 15-18
assorted lines
  drawing 7-9

axes
  drawing 148, 149

B

bar graph
  drawing 162-165
Bezier curve
  drawing 22-24
butt value 6

C

canvas
  converting, to image 115-117
  drawing on 199, 200
canvas API
  beginPath() function 5
  closePath() function 5
  lineCap property 6
  lineTo(x,y) function 5
  lineWidth property 6
  moveTo(x,y) function 5
  stroke() function 5
  strokeStyle property 6
canvas state
  restoring 56-58
  saving 56-58
car movements
  simulating 136-138
Cascaded Style Sheet (CSS)
  about 1, 223
  used, for styling background 224-226
  used, for styling text 224-226
Catapult game 216-222
circles
  drawing 44-46

clear() function 75
clock
   animating 78-83
collision
   demonstrating 207-209
composite operations
   copy (D is ignored 60
   destination-atop (S atop D) 59
   destination-in (S in D) 59
   destination-out (S out D) 59
   destination-over (S over D) 59
   lighter (S plus D) 60
   source-atop (S atop D) 59
   source-in (S in D) 59
   source-out (S out D) 59
   source-over (S over D, default) 59
   xor (S xor D) 60
composites
   demonstrating 59-63
cone
   drawing 179-182
createLinearGradient() method 48
createRadialGradient() method 48
custom shapes and styles
   working with 50-52

D

drag
   about 139
   handling 141
drawLine() function 75
drawTriangle() method 44
drop
   handling 139-141

E

effects
   rendering, to image 105-108
   rendering, to videos 119-122
ellipse
   drawing 55, 56
events
   combining, with animation 142-145

F

flag
   drawing 24-27
frames per second (FPS) 68
Fruit Basket game 212-216

G

game
   deploying, on Android mobile 226-231
gaming states
   about 198
   working 199
gradients
   drawing 46-48
   linear gradient 49
   radial gradient 49
gravity
   demonstrating 71-73

H

horizontal lines
   drawing 7-9
house
   drawing 34-38
HTML5 Canvas
   about 1
   features 1
HTMLPad
   URL 1

I

image
   converting, to canvas 115-117
   cropping 102-104
   drawing 102-104
   effects, rendering 105-108
init() function 75
interoperability 224

J

JavaScript 1
joins
   drawing 10-12

L

line
animating 73-75
drawing 2-6
line graph
drawing 158-161

M

mirror image
drawing 108-110
mouse
drawing 63-66
mouse coordinates
working with 128, 129
mouse event
handling, example 130-132
music
playing 201-203

O

objects
shadows, adding 32, 33

P

panorama
drawing 189-192
particle fountain
animating 90-93
particles
animating 86-89
path
clipping 110-112
Phaser 2.4.4
about 197
reference link 197
physics
demonstrating 210-212
pie chart
drawing 166-168
pixelation 125
point
detecting, in path 133-135

Q

quadratic curve
drawing 19, 20

R

radians 16
rainbow
drawing 21, 22
rain effect
animating 93-96
rectangles
drawing 40-42
reqAnimFrame() function 75
rgb() method 48
rotation
demonstrating 52
round value 6

S

scaling
demonstrating 52-54
shadowBlur property 31
shadowColor property 31
shadowOffsetX property 31
shadowOffsetY property 31
shadows
adding, to objects 32, 33
simple equation
drawing 152-154
sinusoidal wave
drawing 155-157
snow effect
animating 97-100
snowman
drawing 192-196
solar system
animating 83-86
sprite sheet
sprites, using 203-205
square value 6
sublime text
reference link 1

T

text
  animating 76, 77
  drawing 27-29
three.js
  URL 169
torus
  drawing 182-185
touch event
  demonstrating 145, 146
translation
  demonstrating 52
triangles
  drawing 42-44

U

updateLine() function 75

V

vertical lines
  drawing 7-9
videos
  working with 118, 119

W

WebGL 224